Belief Matters

United Methodism's Doctrinal Standards

Charles Yrigoyen, Jr.

ABINGDON PRESS

Nashville

BELIEF MATTERS

This book is printed on acid-free paper.

Library of Congress Cataloging-in-Publication Data

Yrigoyen, Charles, 1937-
    Belief matters: United Methodism's doctrinal standards / Charles Yrigoyen, Jr.
        p. cm.
    ISBN 0-687-09083-0
    1. United Methodist Church (U.S.)—Doctrines.   2. Methodist Church—Doctrines.   I. Title.

BX8331.2.Y95 2001
230'.76—dc21

ISBN 13 978-0-687-09083-9   00-059427

08 09 10—10 9 8 7 6 5 4

MANUFACTURED IN THE UNITED STATES OF AMERICA

For
The "Terrible Twelve":

Charlie and Louise Bartolett
John and Nancy McEllhenney
Dale and Patti Owens
Denny and Lenore Williams
Bob and Mannie Wright

Who have embraced Jean and me
with Wesleyan love for thirty-five years

CONTENTS

PREFACE

Belief matters! This book is written for two purposes. The first is to remind us that *what we believe does matter*. The second is to explain the doctrinal standards of The United Methodist Church—*matters of our belief.*

I have been a Methodist all my life. I was raised in a Methodist parsonage. My father, an outstanding Methodist pastor and preacher, and my mother, a faithful Sunday school teacher, choir member, and active church member, taught me and my brother to love and appreciate the church from our earliest days. The nurture I received in Sunday school, at church camps, in the Methodist Youth Fellowship, and in the company of countless young people and adults made the church the most important place where I have met God. It was in the MYF in 1957 that I met; fell in love with; and later married my wife, Jean, the most supportive and caring companion I can imagine throughout my adult life.

God's call into the ordained ministry of The Methodist Church in 1958 was another high moment in my life. To serve as pastor of local churches; to be in campus ministry; to teach in a United Methodist college; and finally to be in ministry with one of the denomination's general agencies, the General Commission on Archives and History, are gifts of which I have not been worthy.

In every place I have been, I have benefited from the wisdom and ministry of men, women, and young people who are committed to Christ and the church. I have been taught by many people. They are too numerous to mention, and I must resist the temptation to name many of them here.

In light of these comments, you will know why the subject of this book means so much to me. I do not pretend to approach it dispassionately. United Methodism's doctrinal standards are the food of my spiritual and intellectual life. I learn from them, and I cherish the opportunity to discuss them with others as I am doing here.

Several persons do deserve special mention. Kenneth J. Collins, Scott J. Jones, J. Steven O'Malley, and Kenneth E. Rowe are friends and insightful students of our United Methodist tradition. They have read various parts of this book and offered valuable comments and suggestions. The remaining faults and flaws are purely my responsibility.

Finally, I offer this book to ten people who have a special place in our lives. For more than thirty-five years, we twelve have met together as a "reading group" to discuss books, denominational news, and conference gossip. With them we have experienced the joy and pain that people share in genuine friendship as our pastoral appointments, families, and other circumstances have changed. My wish is that others would have a similar gift of thoughtful and supportive friendship.

Charles Yrigoyen, Jr.
Lent, 2000

INTRODUCTION

The date was Monday, June 25, 1744. The place was the Methodist chapel in London that John Wesley had converted from an old cannon factory. They called it "the Foundery." Six persons were meeting, including John and Charles Wesley. Although they did not know it at the time, this was to be the first Methodist "annual conference." After a time of prayer, an agenda for the meeting was decided. They agreed to consider three basic questions: "1. What to teach; 2. How to teach; and, 3. What to do, that is, how to regulate [their] doctrine, discipline, and practice."[1] The answer to each of these questions was critical to the shape of the infant Methodist movement and its future.

During the following days, this "conference" considered a number of important theological topics, including the doctrine of justification by faith, repentance, assurance, sanctification and the holy life, Christian perfection, the nature of the church, how they should organize their ministry, and whether they should leave the Church of England to form a new church. The matter of doctrine, what they should teach, was at the top of their agenda. Why? They believed that doctrine informs our thinking, speaking, and acting. It is an essential part of who we are and what we do.

What *do* we believe? What *should* we believe? These questions are often asked by United Methodists who are seeking to determine the specific doctrines advanced by their church that they can affirm and use as a basic framework of belief for their understanding and practice of the Christian faith.

What is doctrine? The word *doctrine* comes from the Latin term *docere*, which means "to teach." Christian doctrine refers to what the Christian church has generally agreed upon as those teachings that are essential to the identity of God's people. These teachings are rooted in the Bible and have been taught by the church over the centuries. Doctrine is found in the writings of women and men who have attempted to interpret the Bible faithfully and in statements of the church that summarize Christian beliefs, such as the Apostles', Nicene, and other creeds and affirmations (for examples, see *The United Methodist Hymnal*, 880–86). United

Methodists share with other Christians a common heritage of the traditional teachings of the church. The four official doctrinal standards of United Methodism illustrate that it stands in the mainstream of Christian teaching, even though there are some aspects of these traditional teachings that United Methodists have chosen to emphasize. We will consider more about this point in the chapters that follow.

Doctrine is important for several reasons. **(1) Doctrine helps us to understand the biblical message in a clearer, holistic, more organized way.** Doctrine works with the scriptural text to develop ideas that are true and consistent with the Bible's message and intelligible for our belief. For example, the Christian church holds to the doctrine of a trinitarian God; that is, God is one but known in three persons: Father, Son, and Holy Spirit. This doctrine was formulated in the church through the careful study of the Bible and the need to decide answers to such questions as, Who is Jesus and what is his relationship to God? and, Who is the Holy Spirit? After a long period of searching the Scriptures, the church concluded that the trinitarian doctrine of God was the most sensible and faithful way to understand the nature and work of God.

To develop doctrinal statements is not to say that we can always capture in words and phrases all that there is to know about God, God's love, the nature of evil in the world, and the depth of our own sinfulness, to name but a few areas. As we wrestle with these and other subjects related to our faith, we need to allow for the element of mystery. Nevertheless, doctrine helps us understand what we believe.

(2) Doctrine provides a basis for our life. Christianity is more than doctrine. It is our relationship to the triune God whose grace forgives, renews, maintains, and moves us to worship and serve. Doctrine seeks to illuminate that relationship. It secures us to a basic body of teachings that instruct us for faithful, intelligent, effective, and joyful living. The more deeply we understand the biblical faith and let it inform what we think, say, and do, the more it anchors our lives and moves us to serve God and our neighbors. We are what we believe.

(3) Doctrine is necessary for the communication of our faith. The Mormons and Jehovah's Witnesses who come to our doors teach doctrines that are quite different from those of the mainstream of Christianity (for example, Eastern Orthodoxy, Roman Catholicism, and Protestantism). Those who are Muslim, Buddhist, and Jewish also hold to doctrinal beliefs that are quite different from those of Christians. Furthermore, there are many people who live in our communities, with whom we work and shop, who have little or no understanding of our faith. It is impossible to understand the beliefs of others or to speak with them about our faith without employing doctrine. One of the writers of the New Testament advised that we should always be ready to give an account of our faith gently and reverently (1 Peter 3:15-16). If we take seriously opportunities to share our faith with others, in defending what we believe and hoping that they will be captured by God's overwhelming saving grace as we are, doctrine will be an indispensable instrument.

(4) Doctrine is a basis for Christian community and fellowship with our brothers and sisters in Christ. Doctrine is not merely a set of personal beliefs. It is also the basis for our worship, preaching, teaching, and ministry as the body of Christ. Our hymns contain doctrine. We sing them *together*. Our prayers assume a doctrinal understanding of God. We pray them *together*. Pastors and teachers speak to us about doctrine based in Scripture and its application for our circumstances. We listen to them *together*. Biblical faith is personal but not private. We live with other Christians. We worship in community. We share our joys and concerns with them. We serve God and our neighbors in a fellowship of others who are also committed to do the same. Common doctrinal beliefs are a foundation for the Christian community in which we participate.

(5) The official doctrine of the church also protects us from false and subversive teachings. The news media have brought to our attention persons and groups who advance strange and even bizarre religious ideas and practices. Some of them teach racial superiority in the name of God. Others claim that all the Christian churches are wrong and that their leader possesses special and unique insight into the Bible. To know the truth, they say, we need to join the community of their leader. To know what our church teaches, and why, will assist us in recognizing deceitful and dangerous teaching. It will keep us from tumbling into unhealthy extremes.

The United Methodist Church has an official body of doctrine that has historically been deemed important to its life and ministry. There are at least four places in *The Book of Discipline of The United Methodist Church*[2] where reference is made to these doctrinal teachings. First, in the denomination's Constitution there is a section titled "Restrictive Rules." The Articles in this section limit the power of the General Conference, the official legislative body of the church. The first Restrictive Rule reads, "The General Conference shall not revoke, alter, or change our Articles of Religion or establish any new standards or rules of doctrine contrary to our present existing and established standards of doctrine." Here is a clear statement that there are "existing and established standards of doctrine" (*Book of Discipline*; Para. 16) in The United Methodist Church that have been legislatively designated and protected.

Second, when persons seek to become clergy members of a United Methodist annual conference, they are required by the *Discipline* to answer several important historic questions that are to be interpreted and addressed to them by the bishop. Among these questions are the following: "(8) Have you studied the doctrines of The United Methodist Church? (9) After full examination, do you believe that our doctrines are in harmony with the Holy Scriptures?" (*Book of Discipline*; Para. 327). Candidates are obviously expected to answer in the affirmative. Other questions in the series ask about specific doctrinal matters. For example, the candidates are asked if they "expect to be made perfect in love in this life" (*Book of Discipline*; Para. 327). This question refers to the Wesleyan doctrine of Christian perfection that we will have occasion to speak about later in this book. These questions assume the existence of a body of United Methodist doctrine.

Third, the *Discipline* provides that a bishop, clergy member of an annual conference, local pastor, or diaconal minister may be charged with "dissemination of doctrines contrary to the established standards of doctrine of The United Methodist Church" (*Book of Discipline*; Para. 2624.1f). The assumption here is that there are official United Methodist doctrines. Anyone who circulates views opposed to the official doctrine of the church will be held responsible for such acts and, if found guilty, will suffer the appropriate consequences.

Fourth, there is an important section of *The Book of Discipline* titled "Doctrinal Standards and Our Theological Task" (*Book of Discipline*; Paras. 60–63). It is subdivided into sections: "Our Doctrinal Heritage," "Our Doctrinal History," "Our Doctrinal Standards and General Rules," and "Our Theological Task." This is a very important section of our *Discipline*. In addition to describing the historical background of our doctrine, and before we are urged to engage in the work of theology, the four "doctrinal standards" of the church are mentioned. Regrettably, many, perhaps most, United Methodists know very little about this part of the *Discipline*. It is likely that they are unacquainted with the basic body of doctrine that has informed the church's life for the past two centuries.

We are not the first generation to pay little attention to these "doctrinal standards." The "doctrinal standards" have been neglected in other eras in our history. Recent theological bickering and confusion in the denomination, however, have forced many to take a new look at our doctrinal standards and to ask what they can teach us today.

The four chapters that follow are an attempt to describe our four "doctrinal standards" and to explore their meaning for our time. The four are: (1) John Wesley's *Explanatory Notes Upon the New Testament*; (2) the Standard Sermons of John Wesley; (3) the Articles of Religion of The Methodist Church; and (4) the Confession of Faith of The Evangelical United Brethren Church.

Each chapter follows a format that includes four sections:

(1) Historical Background—a description of the origins and development of each doctrinal standard
(2) Content—a narration of the major emphases of each
(3) Assessment—an analysis of the relevance of the doctrinal standard for our time
(4) Conclusion—brief summary comments

At the end of each chapter are annotated suggestions for further reading and study followed by some questions for personal and group reflection and discussion.

In the first two chapters, there is generous use of the hymns of Charles Wesley (1707–1788), brother of Methodism's founder and one of the great poets of Christian history. Charles is believed to have written at least 6,500 hymns, a few of which (too few, unfortunately) remain in church hymnals to this day. We must remember that the hymnal in early Methodism functioned as an unofficial teacher of doctrine. In 1780, John Wesley published a hymnal for his Methodist people titled *A Collection of Hymns, for the Use of the People Called Methodists.*[3] In the Preface he wrote:

> It is not so large as to be either cumbersome or expensive. And it is large enough to contain such a variety of hymns as will not soon be worn threadbare. It is large enough to contain all the important truths of our most holy religion, whether speculative or practical; yea, to illustrate them all, and to prove them both by Scripture and reason. . . . So that this book is in effect a little body of experimental and practical divinity.

The doctrines about which John Wesley wrote were sung by Methodists in the hymns written by his brother. The hymns in our *United Methodist Hymnal* teach doctrine in their own special way as well.

In the Conclusion of the book, we will summarize the main emphases of United Methodism's doctrinal standards and speak about the necessity of "our theological task." Our hope is that the reader will know that there are doctrinal standards in our denomination and will also have an appreciation for their content and usefulness. A glossary of terms used in the book is appended.

SUGGESTIONS FOR FURTHER READING AND STUDY

Abraham, William J. *Waking From Doctrinal Amnesia*. Nashville: Abingdon Press, 1995. Discusses the importance of doctrine and doctrinal standards for United Methodism.

Campbell, Ted A. *Methodist Doctrine: The Essentials*. Nashville: Abingdon Press, 1999. Offers a clear and concise description of the historic teachings of four Methodist denominations—The African Methodist Episcopal Church, The African Methodist Episcopal Zion Church, The Christian Methodist Episcopal Church, and The United Methodist Church.

Gunther, Stephen N., Scott J. Jones, Ted A. Campbell, Rebekah L. Miles, and Randy L. Maddox. *Wesley and the Quadrilateral: Renewing the Conversation*. Nashville: Abingdon Press, 1997. Essays that discuss the role of Scripture, tradition, reason, and experience in Wesleyan theology.

Knight, Henry H. III and Don E. Saliers. *The Conversation Matters: Why United Methodists Should Talk With One Another*. Nashville: Abingdon Press, 1999. Acknowledges theological diversity in The United Methodist Church and discusses the importance of dealing with doctrine in a "conferencing" manner.

Langford, Thomas A. *Doctrine and Theology in The United Methodist Church*. Nashville: Abingdon Press, 1991. A series of essays by leading thinkers on United Methodism's doctrinal standards and theological statements.

McEllhenney, John G., editor. *United Methodism in America: A Compact History*. Nashville: Abingdon Press, 1992. A short survey of the denomination's history in the United States.

Maddox, Randy L., editor. *Rethinking Wesley's Theology for Contemporary Methodism*. Nashville: Abingdon Press, 1998. A series of essays on various topics relating Wesleyan theology to contemporary issues.

Yrigoyen, Charles, Jr. and Susan E. Warrick. *Historical Dictionary of Methodism*. Lanham, MD: Scarecrow Press, 1996. Brief encyclopedic articles on personalities, theological concepts, and the historical development of Methodism. Also contains extended bibliography.

Yrigoyen, Charles, Jr. *John Wesley: Holiness of Heart and Life*. Nashville:

Abingdon Press, 1999. Introduction to Wesley's life and theology with study guide for personal and group use.

---

[1] From *Minutes of Some Late Conversations between the Rev. Mr. Wesleys and Others*, in *The Works of John Wesley*, Volume VIII (Baker Book House, 1979); Conversation I.

[2] All quotations from *The Book of Discipline*, unless otherwise indicated, are from *The Book of Discipline of The United Methodist Church, 1996* (Copyright © 1996 The United Methodist Publishing House).

[3] All quotations from *A Collection of Hymns*, unless otherwise indicated, are from *A Collection of Hymns, for the Use of the People Called Methodists*, in *The Works of John Wesley*, Volume 7, edited by Franz Hildebrandt and Oliver A. Beckerlegge (Abingdon Press, 1983).

CHAPTER 1
JOHN WESLEY'S EXPLANATORY NOTES UPON THE NEW TESTAMENT

John Wesley's *Explanatory Notes Upon the New Testament*[1] are probably the least known and read of the official doctrinal standards of The United Methodist Church. There are at least three reasons for this situation. First, their length (more than one thousand pages in one recent printing) makes it impossible to include them in editions of *The Book of Discipline of The United Methodist Church* where they would be available to a larger number of the church's constituency. Second, copies of the *Notes* are not readily accessible. The superb Bicentennial Edition of *The Works of John Wesley* will have a two-volume critical edition of the *Notes*, but those volumes will not be published for some time and will unfortunately have a more limited circulation than they deserve. In the meantime, reprint editions of the *Notes* are available if one searches diligently. Third, since the *Notes* were first published more than two centuries ago, it is likely that many feel their insights and value have been surpassed by more recent biblical commentaries. Nevertheless, the *Notes* are still considered by United Methodism to be so important as to be listed among its four definitive doctrinal documents.

HISTORICAL BACKGROUND

The *Notes* have long been regarded as a standard exposition of Methodist teaching and preaching. Their significance may be traced to 1763 when John Wesley published the "Model Deed" for Methodist chapels and meeting places. In this deed he stated that the trustees of those properties were to allow only those preachers in their pulpits who proclaimed "no other doctrine than is contained in Mr. W's *Notes Upon the New Testament* and four volumes of *Sermons*."[2] In the centuries that have followed, Methodists have given the *Sermons* and *Notes* a special place.

When we begin to think about our Christian faith, where do we start?

Where can we find guidance for who we are and what we are called to do? Wesley was convinced that the place to begin was the Bible. It is the primary source for our understanding and practice of the Christian faith and the decisive authority in all theological matters. For that reason the founder of Methodism was concerned that Methodists become thoroughly familiar with the Bible. All Christians, he held, should be grounded in the biblical message. Wesley drew his own beliefs from the Bible and found direction for his life there. He wrote, "I receive the written Word as the whole and sole rule of my faith."[3] Wesley's devotion to the Bible began n the Epworth parsonage where, as a child, he had been taught the significance of the biblical message by his parents. His appreciation for the importance of Scripture continued through adolescence and adulthood. Reflecting on his days as a teacher at Oxford University and as a participant in a small religious group of university students known as the Holy Club, he described their mutual commitment to read and study the Bible:

> From the very beginning, from the time that four young men united together, each of them was *homo unius libri*—a man of one book. God taught them all to make his 'Word a lantern unto their feet, and a light to their paths.' They had one, and only one rule of judgment with regard to all their tempers, words, and actions, namely, the oracles of God. They were one and all determined to be *Bible-Christians*. They were continually reproached for this very thing; some terming them in derision *Bible-bigots;* others[,] *Bible-moths*—feeding, they said, upon the Bible as moths do upon cloth. And indeed to this day it is their constant endeavour to think and speak as the oracles of God.[4] ("On God's Vineyard," *Works*; Vol. 3, page 504)

In one sense Wesley's words are deceptive. He was a "man of many books," an avid reader throughout his life, whose reading included a wide range of subjects. In another sense Wesley was right. The one book that he used to measure his faith and life more than any other was the Bible. The Bible was most important because he was convinced that reading, studying, and living the biblical message draw us deeper into God's presence and love and equip us for the life God intends us to live.

Never content simply to exhort Methodists to use the Bible as a means by which God informed, instructed, and inspired its readers, Wesley set forth a plan for reading and studying the Scripture. It is advisable, he wrote:

(1) To set apart a little time, if you can, every morning and evening for that purpose. (2) At each time . . . to read a chapter out of the Old, and one out of the New, Testament. If you cannot do this, to take a single chapter, or part of one. (3) To read this with a single eye, to know the whole will of God, and have a fixed resolution to do it. In order to know his will, you should, (4) Have a constant eye to the analogy of faith, the connection and harmony there is between those grand, fundamental doctrines of original sin, justification by faith, the new birth, [and] inward and outward holiness. (5) Serious and earnest prayer should be constantly used before we consult the oracles of God; seeing "Scripture can only be understood through the same Spirit whereby it was given." Our reading should likewise be closed with prayer, that what we read may be written on our hearts.

(6) It might also be of use if, while we read, we were frequently to pause and examine ourselves by what we read, both with regard to our hearts and lives. This would furnish us with matter of praise, where we found God had enabled us to conform to his blessed will; and a matter of humiliation, where we are conscious of having fallen short. And whatever light you receive should be used to the uttermost, and that immediately. Let there be no delay. Whatever you resolve, begin to execute the first moment you can. So shall you find this word to be indeed the power of God unto present and eternal salvation.[5]

Wesley's writings, which include a published journal of his daily activities, sermons, letters, books, pamphlets, and hymnbooks, are saturated with biblical ideas and quotations. He was committed to teaching the Bible at every opportunity. This commitment is evident in his publishing commentaries on the Old and New Testaments, which he called *Explanatory Notes Upon the Old Testament* and *Explanatory Notes Upon the New Testament*.

In 1755, Wesley published the first edition of his *Explanatory Notes Upon the New Testament*. He began to write them on January 6, 1754, in Bristol, England, when he suffered through a period of illness that prevented him from engaging in his normal schedule of vigorous itinerant preaching. In spite of his illness, he worked diligently on this project daily for six weeks from 5:00 AM until 9:00 PM, except for meals and a little rest. The result was his own translation of the New Testament from the Greek language (We often forget that Wesley was a skillful student of the biblical languages, especially Greek.) and comments on the biblical text for almost every verse in the New Testament. When this project was published, the biblical text was printed at the top of each page and the commentary was placed at the bottom. It was an ambitious undertaking. The first printed edition was more than 750 pages. Within a few years these *Notes* occupied a unique place in the life of the Methodist people. The *Notes* were regularly used by Wesley's people, especially his preachers, as a guide for reading, interpreting, and proclaiming the New Testament message.

In the important Preface to the *Notes*, Wesley described the audience for whom they were intended. He wrote that the *Notes*

> were not principally designed for [people] of learning, who are provided with many other helps; and much less for [people] of long and deep experience in the ways and word of God. I desire to sit at their feet, and to learn [from] them. But I write chiefly for plain unlettered [people], who understand only their mother-tongue, and yet reverence and love the word of God, and have a desire to save their souls.

The *Notes* for these "plain" people were designed to accomplish at least four main purposes. **(1)** They were meant to encourage Christians to read the Bible and to think about the biblical message. Although not doctrinal standards for United Methodists, in 1765, Wesley published *Explanatory Notes Upon the Old Testament* containing more than 2,600 pages and bound in three volumes. Unlike the New Testament *Notes*, only one edition of the Old Testament commentary was published. In the Preface to the Old Testament volume, Wesley stated his attitude about the significance of the biblical message. He wrote, "It is not my design to write a book which [someone] may read separate from the Bible; but barely to assist those who fear God, in hearing and reading the Bible itself, by showing the natural sense of every part, in as few and plain words as I can." He continued, "It is no part of my design to save either learned or unlearned [people] from the trouble of thinking. If so, I might perhaps write [volumes] too, which usually overlay, rather than help the thought. On the contrary, my intention is, to make them think, and assist them in thinking." The New Testament *Notes*, no less than those for the Old Testament, were meant to encourage faithful people to read the Bible and to think, that is, to interact with the biblical text and to practice its message.

(2) The *Notes* were written to illuminate the central message of the New Testament. Wesley was interested in every New Testament verse; but he believed that together they dealt with one main theme: the desperate condition of human beings estranged from God and one another and the gracious actions of the triune God to bring new life and direction to individuals and the human community. For Wesley, as we noted above, Scripture principally deals with "original sin, justification by faith, new birth, [and] inward and outward holiness."[6] These themes pervade Wesley's commentaries, sermons, and other writings. In this chapter the biblical citations in parentheses, for example (Romans 5:14), refer to comments in his *Notes*.

(3) Wesley also intended the *Notes* to explain and clarify the biblical text. Some words, phrases, concepts, and events in the Bible would be better understood by readers if they were supplied with an appropriate definition or other comment. For example, commenting on Matthew 27:26, which describes Jesus being delivered to be crucified, Wesley graphically narrated the procedure for crucifying someone in the first century. His comment was:

> The person crucified was nailed to the cross as it lay on the ground, through each hand extended to the utmost stretch, and through both the feet together. Then the cross was raised up, and the foot of it thrust with a violent shock into a hole in the ground prepared for it. This shock disjointed the body, whose whole weight hung upon the nails, till the person expired through mere dint of pain. This kind of death was used only by the Romans, and by them inflicted only on slaves and the vilest criminals. (Matthew 27:26, *Notes*)

In explaining and clarifying the biblical text, Wesley attempted to avoid lengthy and complicated comments. That was his plan from the beginning. He wrote in the Preface to the *Notes*:

> I have endeavored to make the notes as short as possible that the comment may not obscure or swallow up the text; and as plain as possible, in pursuance of my main design, to assist the unlearned reader. For this reason I have studiously avoided, not only all curious and critical inquiries, and all use of the learned languages [i.e., Greek and Hebrew], but all such methods of reasoning and modes of experience as people in common life are unacquainted with. (Preface, *Notes*)

It must be mentioned here that Wesley consulted the work of other New Testament students and commentators in composing his *Notes*. He especially mentioned the Lutheran scholar John Albert Bengel (1687–1752), on whom he depended heavily, and also John Heylyn (1685?–1759), John Guyse (died 1761), and Philip Doddridge (1702–1751).

In addition to what he learned from these and other biblical commentators, Wesley drew substantially from his own study of the Scripture, meditation, preaching, and experience. The result was a blending of the work that he considered the best scholarship of his day with his own theological insights. Even with the help of able commentators and with his own rigorous study, however, there were places where Wesley confessed that he found passages difficult to understand. Not surprisingly, one New Testament book that he found a problem was Revelation. In his introductory comments on the book he wrote, "I by no means pretend to understand or explain all that is contained in this mysterious book. I only offer what help I can to the serious inquirer, and shall rejoice if any be moved thereby more carefully to read and more deeply to consider the words of this prophecy."

(4) Wesley also wanted the *Notes* to emphasize the biblical message in a way that inspired and challenged readers. He believed that God speaks through the scriptural text to move the reader to love and serve God and neighbor more faithfully. For example, in Acts 15:36, Paul addresses his companion Barnabas saying that they should go to every city where they had preached to see how their Christian friends are doing. Wesley commented that Paul meant that he and Barnabas should go to see "how their souls prosper; how they grow in faith, hope, love." Then Wesley added, "What else ought to be the grand and constant inquiry in every ecclesiastical visitation? Reader, how dost thou do?"

Although Wesley's comments were directed to both lay and clergy readers, a number of his comments were directed specifically to the clergy. For example, he wrote that the clergy "ought to lay before the Lord, in prayer, the obedience or disobedience of their hearers" (Luke 14:21, *Notes*). The role of the clergy is to help their people go "forward in faith and holiness" (2 Corinthians 2:24, *Notes*). In his comments on Acts 8:30, Wesley pointed out that Philip's sermon "did not begin about the weather, news, or the like. In speaking for God, we may frequently come to the point at once, without circumlocution." This was a biting criticism of those clergy whose sermons did not move directly to the heart of the Christian message but instead dealt with peripheral matters.

CONTENT

Biblical commentaries are not intended to be complete and detailed systems of Christian doctrine. They usually move through the chapters and verses of the books of the Bible explaining the meaning of a verse or series of verses. The commentator tries to help the reader understand what the original writer meant and how that applies to the reader's life.

Wesley's *Explanatory Notes Upon the New Testament* follows this pattern. It does not pretend to touch upon every facet of the Christian faith. However, the *Notes* do reveal some of the main themes of Wesley's theology and the major historic theological emphases of Methodism. The three prominent themes are the human situation apart from God, the saving work of God, and the Christian life of holiness.

(1) The Human Situation Apart From God

There was no question for Wesley that God is the "Author and Creator" of everything. By God's "sole command" all things in heaven and on earth were "[f]ormed, fashioned, and finished" including, of course, the human race (Hebrews 11:3, *Notes*). The human community was created to live at peace with itself and with God and to be blessed by God's presence and gifts.

Humans, however, chose to live otherwise. They revolted against God's purpose, specifically in the person of Adam (Romans 5:14, *Notes*), whom the Scripture refers to as the "first man." So, from the beginning, the human will was set against God. This rebellion, which the New Testament writers call "sin," involves all of us. It is the condition in which we live, every one of us. It is alienation from one another and from God, a refusal to recognize, worship, and serve our Maker. In Wesley's words it is "unbelief." He wrote, "Unbelief is the parent of all evil, and the very essence of unbelief lies in *departing from God*, as *the living God*—The fountain of all our life, holiness, [and] happiness" (Hebrews 3:12, *Notes*).

The sinful state in which we live manifests itself in all sorts of ways in the life of individuals and in the human community. Wesley was not at a loss to catalog the evidences of the sinful condition that he found well described in the New Testament. These evidences encompass specific thoughts, words, and actions that hurt our neighbors and deny God's presence, power, and purpose. These evidences include "cruelty, inhumanity, and all malevolent affections" (Mark 7:22, *Notes*) such as captivity to the "desire of the flesh," the "desire of the eye," whereby we idolize "whatever is grand, new, or beautiful" and "the pride of life" (1 John 2:16, *Notes*). They involve "all that pomp in clothes, houses, furniture, equipage, manner of living, which generally procure honor from the bulk of mankind, and so gratify pride and vanity. It therefore directly includes the desire of praise, and, remotely, covetousness. All these desires are not from God, but from the prince of this world" (1 John 2:16, *Notes*). They pervert our relationship with God and our neighbors.

Those who choose to live in this state are "rebels against [God], deniers of his providence," and are at enmity with God's "justice and holiness" (Romans 1:30, *Notes*). They are inventors of "new pleasures, new ways of gain, new acts of hurting [others], particularly in war" (Romans 1:30, *Notes*), which turn attention away from God, the true focus of life.

There is a price to be paid for living a life of unbelief. When we live apart from God, denying his presence, refusing to worship him, failing to serve him, and ignoring the needs of our neighbors, we live under the power of sin and are turned aside from the full blessing and joy that God intends for each and all of us. We refuse to receive the goodness and joy of life that God wants to give.

Furthermore, the life of unbelief is lived under God's judgment and wrath. Wesley was not reluctant to speak about the anger of God kindled against those who rebel against him. Wesley held that "God's eternal, essential righteousness" includes justice and condemns sin (Romans 1:17, *Notes*). So, those who neglect or repudiate God are subject to divine condemnation (James 2:12), death ("the devil's servant and serjeant") (Hebrews 2:14, *Notes*), and eternal torment (Matthew 25:46, *Notes*). That is not what God wants; it is the result of human choice.

Charles Wesley warned of the danger of living apart from God and asked why we would choose to live that way. Here are words from one of his hymns:

> Sinners, turn, why will you die?
>   God, your Maker, asks you why.
> God, who did your being give,
>   Made you himself, that you might live;
> He the fatal cause demands,
>   Asks the work of his own hands,
> Why, you thankless creatures, why
>   Will you cross his love and die?
>
> Sinners, turn, why will you die?
>   God, your Saviour, asks you why.
> God, who did your souls retrieve,
>   Died himself that you might live.
> Will you let him die in vain?
>   Crucify your Lord again?
> Why, you ransomed sinners, why
>   Will you slight his grace, and die?
>
> Sinners, turn, why will you die?
>   God the Spirit asks you why.
> He, who all your lives hath strove,
>   Wooed you to embrace his love.

> Will you not his grace receive?
>   Will you still refuse to live?
> Why, you long-sought sinners, why
>   Will you grieve your God, and die?
>
> Dead, already dead within,
>   Spiritually dead in sin,
> Dead to God, while here you breathe,
>   Pant you after second death?
> Will you still in sin remain,
>   Greedy of eternal pain?
> O you dying sinners, why,
>   Why will you for ever die?[7]

(*The United Methodist Hymnal*; 346, stanza 4 from an earlier text)

(2) The Saving Work of God

Wesley was clear about the nature and problem of sin. It disrupts and damages our relationships with God and our neighbors. Sin also, therefore, creates havoc in us. But Wesley was not preoccupied with the destructive effects of sin's idolatry and disobedience. While the sinful state and its result was *bad news*, it was overshadowed by the *good news* of God's action to forgive, reconcile, heal, and create in us new life. Our desperate and dangerous condition apart from God is God's opportunity to demonstrate the breadth and depth of divine love. To put it in Wesley's words, human "extremity is God's opportunity" (Matthew 8:24, *Notes*).

Our hope and salvation are rooted in the grace of God. This is the *good news* for all people. The gracious God is always ready to give us a new beginning. Throughout the *Notes*, Wesley referred to the central importance of divine grace. Grace is God's "glorious, free love" (Ephesians 1:6; Galatians 2:21, *Notes*) and is available to all people "without any respect to human worthiness" (Ephesians 2:8, *Notes*). It is "the source of all our blessings" (Romans 5:21, *Notes*).

Grace is the action of the triune God. Wesley's *Notes* reiterate the trinitarian nature of God. In the *Notes*, Wesley never attempted to provide an extensive definition of the Trinity; but he always affirmed it. He wrote, "The Lord our God, the Lord, the God of all . . . , is one God, essentially, though three persons" (Mark 12:29, *Notes*). This trinitarian understanding of God is interwoven throughout the Scriptures (Luke 4:18; Revelation 4:8, *Notes*). Redemption and new life is the saving work of the trinitarian God (Hebrews 9:14, *Notes*).

Many of Charles Wesley's hymns recognize the redemptive work of the triune God and offer praise for God's creative and redeeming acts. One of them reads:

> Come, Father, Son, and Holy Ghost,
>   One God in Persons Three!
> Bring back the heavenly blessing, lost
>   By all mankind, and me.
>
> Thy favour, and thy nature too,
>   To me, to all restore!
> Forgive, and after God renew,
>   And keep us evermore!
>   (*A Collection of Hymns*; 243)

The person and redemptive work of Jesus are central to the saving work of God. Jesus' life, death, and resurrection are the main events by which reconciliation with God is accomplished. Wesley was persuaded that the traditional description of Jesus in both his complete humanity and complete divinity was scripturally faithful, accurate, and sufficient (Philippians 2:6-11; Colossians 1:15-22, *Notes*). Jesus claimed that he was the long-expected Messiah, the Christ, the Anointed One of God (Matthew 11:4-6, *Notes*). Wesley wrote, "That Jesus is the Christ; that he is the Son of God; that he came in the flesh, is one undivided truth, and [anyone] that denies any part of this, in effect denies the whole" (1 John 2:22, *Notes*).

Following traditional theological categories, Wesley described Jesus as occupying a threefold office. He is prophet, priest, and king (Matthew 1:16; 11:29; Philippians 3:8, *Notes*). As *prophet*, Jesus teaches us who God is and what the will of God is for us. As *priest*, he is the Mediator and Intercessor. By his atoning death on the cross, he "appeased the Father's wrath, obtained pardon and acceptance for us, and, consequently, dissolved the dominion and power which Satan had over us through our sins" (Colossians 1:14, *Notes*). There is a pronounced emphasis in the *Notes* on Jesus as our Atonement and High Priest (for example, Hebrews 2:10, 17; 9:22, 26; 1 John 2:2, *Notes*). Jesus is the Second Adam through whose righteousness we are given new life (Romans 5:14; 1 Corinthians 15:47, *Notes*). Christ alone is our Redeemer and the Savior of the world (Galatians 3:13, *Notes*). As *king*, Jesus has defeated the powers of evil and death. He wants "to reign in our hearts, and subdue all things to himself" (Matthew 1:16, *Notes*). So, Wesley visualizes Jesus imploring each and all of us, "Believe in me; receive me as your prophet, priest, and king" (Matthew 11:29, *Notes*).

Charles Wesley set forth the Wesleyan understanding of the threefold office of Christ in three stanzas of a longer hymn published in 1739:

> Prophet, to me reveal
>   Thy Father's perfect will:
> Never mortal spoke like thee,
>   Human prophet like divine;
> Loud and strong their voices be,
>   Small, and still, and inward thine!
>
> On thee my Priest I call,
>   Thy blood atoned for all:
> Still the Lamb as slain appears,
>   Still thou stand'st before the throne,
> Ever off'ring up my prayers,
>   These presenting with thy own.
>
> Jesu, thou art my King,
>   From thee my strength I bring:
> Shadowed by thy mighty hand,
>   Saviour, who shall pluck me thence?
> Faith supports, by faith I stand,
>   Strong as thy omnipotence.[8]

The sixteenth-century Protestant reformer Martin Luther considered the narrative of Jesus' conversation with Nicodemus in the Gospel of John, Chapter 3, a brief statement of the core of the Christian message. Wesley's comment on the same passage reveals a similar view. He wrote:

> In this solemn discourse our Lord shows that no external profession, no ceremonial ordinances or privileges of birth, could entitle any to the blessings of the Messiah's kingdom; that an entire change of heart, as well as of life, was necessary for that purpose; that this could only be wrought in man by the almighty power of God; that every man born into the world was by nature in a state of sin, condemnation, and misery; that the free mercy of God had given his Son to deliver them from it, and to raise them to a blessed immortality; that all mankind, Gentiles as well as Jews, might share in these benefits, procured by his being lifted up on the cross, and to be received by faith in him; but that, if they rejected him, their eternal, aggravated condemnation would be the certain consequence. (John 3:3, *Notes*)

Wesley was always eager to show that God loves all people and desires that all be forgiven, reconciled, and given new life. God "does not confine his love to one nation; in . . . general . . . he is loving to every [person] and willeth all . . . should be saved" (Acts 10:34, *Notes*). Although Wesley believed that Scripture taught foreknowledge, that is, that God knows all things in advance, there was no room in Wesley's thought for a predestinarian view that denied the freedom of humans to accept or reject God's offer of salvation. Wesley was convinced that Scripture "speaks of God's universal offers of grace; his invitations, promises, threatenings, being all general" (1 Peter 1:2, *Notes*). In his *Notes* and elsewhere in his writings, Wesley ruled out any form of theology, such as Calvinism, which held that some were "elected absolutely and unconditionally to eternal life" while others were "predestinated absolutely and unconditionally to eternal death" (1 Corinthians 9:27, *Notes*). Such predestination, which denied free will to human beings, is not the teaching of the Bible when it is read as a whole.

By God's grace all are free to decide for or against God. All are invited to choose life by receiving God's forgiveness in faith, or they must suffer the consequences. Wesley did not make as clear in the *Notes* as he did elsewhere that the source of our freedom is what he called "preventing" or prevenient grace (but see his comments on Acts 13:48 and Romans 2:14). Prevenient grace awakens us to the chasm that exists between what God expects us to be and what we really are. It convinces us of our need of God's forgiveness and stirs us to repentance. For Wesley repentance is not merely "a thorough conviction of sin," but "a change of heart (and consequently of life) from . . . sin to . . . holiness" (Matthew 3:8, *Notes*). By God's grace we are moved to trust God's pardon and forgiveness demonstrated in Christ's life, death, and resurrection. That is what the Bible calls justification by faith. It is to be "pardoned and accepted by God upon our believing, for the sake of what Christ has done and suffered" (Romans 4:9, *Notes*). In his comment on Romans 4:5, Wesley described the process of this justification:

> For the sinner, being first convinced of his sin and danger by the Spirit of God, stands trembling before the awful tribunal of divine justice; and has nothing to plead, but his own guilt, and the merits of a Mediator. Christ here interposes; justice is satisfied [by Christ's atoning death]; the sin is remitted, and pardon is applied to the soul, by a divine faith wrought by the Holy Ghost.

The sinner's pardon (justification) is accompanied by new birth whereby the believer is "inwardly changed from all sinfulness to all holiness" (John 3:7, *Notes*). This is called new birth "because as great a change . . . passes on the soul as passes on the body when it is born into the world" (John 3:7, *Notes*). In another passage Wesley extended his commentary on the effects of the new birth on the sinner:

He has new life, new senses, new faculties, new affections, new appetites, new ideas and conceptions. His whole tenor of action and conversation is new, and he lives, as it were, in a new world. God, [neighbor], . . . earth, and all therein, appear in a new light, and stand related to him in a new manner, since he was created anew in Christ Jesus. (2 Corinthians 5:17, *Notes*)

Those who have been forgiven and granted new life also receive the Holy Spirit, who assures them of their status as children of God. Wesley affirmed that all Christians are given the Holy Spirit (1 Corinthians 12:3, *Notes*) whose "inward, powerful testimony" of our safe standing with God is also accompanied by the various gifts that the Spirit brings to our lives (1 Peter 1:12, *Notes*). Some of these spiritual gifts are listed in Romans 12 and in 1 Corinthians 12. Those who receive the Spirit also bear the Spirit's fruits, such as love, joy, peace, gentleness, goodness, fidelity in relationships, and temperance (Galatians 5:22-23, *Notes*). Several of Charles Wesley's hymns speak of the Spirit's assurance, gifts, and fruits. One of them follows:

How can we sinners know
Our sins on earth forgiven?
How can my gracious Saviour show
My name inscribed in heaven?

What we have felt and seen
With confidence we tell,
And publish to the ends of earth
The signs infallible.

We by his Spirit prove
And know the things of God,
The things which freely of his love
He hath on us bestowed.

His Spirit to us he gave,
And dwells in us, we know;

The witness in ourselves we have,
    And all his fruits we show.

The meek and lowly heart,
    That in our Saviour was,
To us that Spirit doth impart,
    And signs us with his cross.

Our nature's turned, our mind
    Transformed in all its powers;
And both the witnesses are joined,
    The Spirit of God with ours.

Whate'er our pardoning Lord
    Commands, we gladly do,
And guided by his sacred Word
    We all his steps pursue.

His glory our design,
    We live our God to please;
And rise, with filial fear divine,
    To perfect holiness.
(*The United Methodist Hymnal*; 372)

At its close this Wesleyan hymn points to the culmination of the process of God's saving work. The process begins with creation and prevenient grace and continues through repentance, forgiveness (justification by faith), new birth, and assurance. The goal of this process is a holy life.

(3) The Christian Life of Holiness

The emphasis on living a holy life is prominent in all the writings of John Wesley, and the *Notes* are no exception. He believed that holiness is a central message of the Bible. In commenting on the speech of Zacharias, the father of John the Baptist, where Zacharias said we are to serve God in holiness and righteousness all our lives, Wesley wrote, "Here is the substance of the great promise. That we shall be always holy, always happy; that being delivered from Satan and sin, from every uneasy and unholy temper, we shall joyfully love and serve God, in every thought, word, and work" (Luke 1:74, *Notes*).

Wesley was unremitting in his criticism of those who claimed to be Christians but who did not live the holy life. Holiness is the badge of their salvation. Persons who shun holy living are not genuinely God's people (Galatians 2:18, *Notes*). While they might be content with keeping a few religious observances, such as celebrating religious holidays or engaging in certain religious practices, they lack the life of holy righteousness that is the mark of authentic Christian faith. "Real religion," Wesley wrote, "does *not* consist in words [only], *but in the power of God* ruling the heart" (1 Corinthians 4:20, *Notes*). We should always be holy in our actions (Matthew 13:28, *Notes*). Wesley described some who call themselves Christians, but are not holy, as "darnel" (grass that grows as a weed among corn) (Matthew 13:28, *Notes*). They have a form of godliness, he said, without the evidence and power (Matthew 10:28, *Notes*).

What is holiness? What does it mean to be holy? The holy life that God intends for each and all involves two dimensions. **(1)** It is loving God with all that we are and have. **(2)** Holiness is also loving our neighbor as ourselves. For Wesley the neighbor was everyone, even our enemies. These two, love of God and love of neighbor, are inseparable. It is important to say something about each of them.

First, to be holy is to love God. Wesley, of course, understood the basic nature of God to be love. Commenting on 1 John 4:8, "God is love," Wesley wrote:

> This little sentence brought St. John more sweetness, even in the time he was writing it, than the whole world can bring. God is often styled holy, righteous, wise; but not holiness, righteousness, or wisdom in the abstract, as he is said to be love; intimating that this is his darling, his reigning attribute, the attribute that sheds an amiable glory on all his other perfections. (1 John 4:8, *Notes*)

Our love for God is possible because we are first loved by God and given the capacity to love. Wesley wrote, "This is the sum of all religion, the genuine model of Christianity. None can say more; why should anyone say less, or less intelligibly" (1 John 4:19, *Notes*).

There are several places in which Wesley describes concretely what it means to love God. For example, loving God includes uniting "all the faculties of [the] soul to render [to God] the most intelligent and sincere, the most affectionate and resolute service" (Luke 10:27; compare Mark 12:33, *Notes*). It involves our embracing, trusting, worshiping, obeying, and serving God.

Second, holiness means to imitate God's love in our relationships with others. Wesley exhorted his readers, "Imitate the God of love" (Matthew 7:11, *Notes*). One of the basic evidences of this imitation is forgiving others continually as God steadfastly forgives us (Luke 11:4; Ephesians 4:32, *Notes*). The nature of divine love we are to copy is, of course, explained in

1 Corinthians 13. Wesley's comments on that passage are extensive and moving. A few of them are especially poignant:

> The love of God, and of our neighbor for God's sake, is patient toward all. . . . It suffers all the weakness, ignorance, errors, and infirmities of the children of God; all the malice and wickedness of the children of the world: and all this, not only for a time, but to the end. And in every step toward overcoming evil with good, it is kind, soft, mild, benign. (1 Corinthians 13:4, *Notes*)

This love never "hastily condemn[s] any one; never passes a severe sentence on a slight or sudden view of things. Nor does it ever act or behave in a violent, headstrong, or precipitate manner" (1 Corinthians 13:4, *Notes*). "It casts out all jealousies, all evil surmises, all readiness to believe evil [of anyone]" (1 Corinthians 13:5, *Notes*). Authentic love endures all "the injustice, the malice, the cruelty" that people can inflict on us because Christ strengthens us to persevere (1 Corinthians 13:7, *Notes*). To imitate God's love is to put on Christ. It is to be in the "most intimate union with him, and being clothed with all the graces which are in him" (Romans 13:14, *Notes*).

Love for our neighbor and, therefore, love for God is exhibited in what Wesley called "works of mercy." These are acts that are evidence in us of "faith working by love" (1 Corinthians 7:19, *Notes*). For example, love is demonstrated in "works of mercy" when we feed the hungry; clothe the naked; and care for the homeless, sick, and imprisoned (Matthew 25:35, *Notes*).

Wesley warned that there are hindrances to holiness, to loving God and others. There are attitudes and acts that not only obstruct the pathway of holiness but may completely destroy it. In general, the most serious obstacle that may derail holiness is desiring anything other than that which leads to God. Wesley did not believe that once we possess saving faith, we may relax and adopt a careless style of life. We are free at any time to abandon God and to forsake the path of holy living.

One of the most serious threats to holy living is the love of money. It is a "snare" that jeopardizes our trust in God (Matthew 6:19, *Notes*). Riches are deceitful.

> They smile, and betray; kiss, and smite into hell. They put out the eyes, harden the heart, steal away all the life of God; fill the soul with pride, anger, love of the world; make [people] enemies to the whole cross of Christ! And all the while are eagerly desired, and

vehemently pursued, even by those who believe there is a God! (Matthew 13:22, *Notes*)

"Rich man, tremble!" Wesley warned. Those who love money do not love God and cannot enter God's kingdom (Matthew 19:24; Mark 10:24, *Notes*).

While there are hindrances along the way of holiness, God provides gifts to encourage us and to keep us on the path. The way of Christ is a disciplined way, a journey of self-denial and cross-bearing that we cannot manage without God's presence, power, and gifts (Matthew 16:24, *Notes*). Among God's gifts are Scripture, prayer, the Lord's Supper, and the fellowship of other Christians, which in many places Wesley called "means of grace" and "works of piety."

The Scriptures (Old and New Testaments) are the major means to instruct us concerning who God is, the futility of life apart from God, God's saving acts to give us new life, and our response to God in faith and holy living. When read with faith and prayer, the Scriptures inspire us to face up to ourselves and our infirmities; to celebrate God's revitalizing grace; and to live in the only way that brings true and lasting happiness, that is, holiness of heart and life (2 Timothy 3:15-16, *Notes*).

Prayer is another indispensable gift. It is "the breath of our spiritual life" (1 Thessalonians 5:16, *Notes*). Just as a person cannot live without breathing, so the person of faith cannot exist without praying. Prayer produces in us a disposition to receive God's "grace and blessing." It exercises "our dependence on God" (Matthew 6:8, *Notes*). Praying is "offering up our desires to God" (1 Timothy 2:1, *Notes*)), including our needs and our intercessions for others (Ephesians 6:18, *Notes*). Whoever prays "is ever giving praise, whether in ease or pain, both for prosperity and for the greatest adversity," since God sees us through both (1 Thessalonians 5:16, *Notes*). Therefore, we should pray without ceasing in private and in public, aloud or silently (Ephesians 6:18, *Notes*). There are, of course, hindrances to prayer. "All sin hinders prayer," Wesley wrote, "particularly anger. Anything [or anyone] at which we are angry is never more apt to come into our mind than when we are at prayer; and those who do not forgive will find no forgiveness with God" (1 Peter 3:7, *Notes*).

The Lord's Supper is yet another of God's gifts that sustains the holy life. It is the successor to the Jewish Passover meal (Matthew 26:26, *Notes*) and reminds us of Jesus' death as the institution of a new covenant with God (Mark 14:24, *Notes*). The Lord's Supper is a memorial, a remembrance of Christ's suffering and dying love on our behalf (1 Corinthians 11:24, *Notes*). But it is more than remembering. It is also the means by which we participate in the "invaluable benefits" of Jesus' sacrificial death and by which we are not only united with Christ but also with one another as we eat bread and drink the cup (1 Corinthians 10:16-17, *Notes*).

Many of Charles Wesley's hymns speak about the significance of the Lord's Supper. One of them reads in part:

> O the depth of love divine,
>> the unfathomable grace!
> Who shall say how bread and wine God
>> into us conveys!
> How the bread his flesh imparts,
>> how the wine transmits
>> his blood,
> Fills his faithful people's hearts
>> with all the life of God!
>
> Let the wisest mortals show how we the grace
>> receive;
> Feeble elements bestow a power not theirs
>> to give.
> Who explains the wondrous way,
>> how through these the virtue
>> came?
> These the virtue did convey,
>> yet still remain the same.
>
> How can spirits heavenward rise,
>> by earthly matter fed,
> Drink herewith divine supplies and eat
>> immortal bread?
> Ask the Father's wisdom how:
>> Christ who did the means ordain;
> Angels round our altars bow to search it
>> out, in vain.
>
> Sure and real is the grace, the manner be
>> unknown;
> Only meet us in thy ways and perfect us in
>> one.
> Let us taste the heavenly powers,
>> Lord, we ask for nothing more.

Thine to bless, 'tis only ours to wonder and
adore.
(*The United Methodist Hymnal*; 627)

The fellowship of other Christians also provides the sustenance that nourishes faith and the holy life. Wesley was impressed with the earliest Christian community described in the Book of Acts. He found it to be "a company of [people], called by the gospel, grafted into Christ by baptism, animated by love, united by all kind of fellowship, and disciplined [by such events as] the death of Ananias and Sapphira," whose demise occurred when they broke covenant with God and the community of their sisters and brothers (Acts 5:10, *Notes*). The daily life of the earliest church was characterized by "1. Hearing the word [through preaching and teaching]: 2. Having all things [in] common: 3. Receiving the Lord's Supper: [and] 4. Prayer" (Acts 2:42, *Notes*). Obviously, Wesley thought these should be important to the daily existence of the church in every age. He was especially interested that the early Christians had all things in common. This, he commented, was not because Christ commanded it, but that love compelled the earliest believers to live in such a fashion. Wesley wrote:

It was a natural fruit of that love wherewith each member of the community loved every other as his own soul. And if the whole Christian church had continued in this spirit, this usage must have continued through all ages. To affirm, therefore, that Christ did not design it should continue, is neither more nor less than to affirm that Christ did not design this measure of love should continue. (Acts 2:45, *Notes*)

The quality of life in the early church was such that the suffering of any of its members was felt by the whole body of believers (Colossians 1:24, *Notes*). The fellowship of other Christians is a necessity and a channel for God to bless those on the path of holiness.

Baptism was important for Wesley. He affirmed the validity of baptizing both infants and adults. Baptism is not merely a ceremony of entrance into the church; it is also a way by which saving grace is conveyed to the recipient. Wesley wrote, "Through the water of baptism we are saved from the sin which overwhelms the world as a flood: *not*, indeed, the bare outward sign, but the inward grace; a divine consciousness that both our persons and our actions are accepted through him who died and rose again for us" (1 Peter 3:21, *Notes*).

The unity of the church was critical for Wesley. He disliked any "uncharitable divisions" in it (1 Corinthians 11:18, *Notes*) and all that "occasions strife and animosities, schisms and parties in the church" (Titus 3:10, *Notes*). We should be wary, he warned, of condemning others who differ with us on those things that do not involve the core of the Christian faith. He urged, "Neither directly nor indirectly discourage or hinder any[one] who brings sinners from the power of Satan to God, 'because he followeth not us,' in opinions, modes of worship, or anything else which does not affect the essence of religion" (Mark 9:39, *Notes*). And, Wesley exhorted, let us never condemn anyone without hearing what they think and have to say (Acts 25:16, *Notes*).

Charles Wesley's hymn "Christ, From Whom All Blessings Flow" speaks of the nature of the church and the significance of unity in it:

> Christ, from whom all blessings flow,
>   Perfecting the saints below,
> Hear us, who thy nature share,
>   Who thy mystic body are.
>
> Join us in one spirit join,
>   Let us still receive of thine;
> Still for more on thee we call,
>   Thou who fillest all in all.
> . . . .
> Sweetly may we all agree,
>   Touched with softest sympathy;
> Kindly for each other care,
>   Every member feel its
>   share.
> . . . .
> Many are we now, and one,
>   We who Jesus have put on;
> There is neither bond nor free,
>   Male nor female, Lord, in thee!
> (*The United Methodist Hymnal*; 550, stanza 3 from an earlier text)

So, the holy (sanctified) life is created, encouraged, and sustained by God's presence and gifts. It should aim at what Wesley called Christian perfection, "the highest degree of holiness" (2 Corinthians 13:11, *Notes*). This is "a state of spiritual [maturity] both in understanding and strength" (Ephesians 4:13, *Notes*). It is the faithful life "adorned with every Christian grace" (James 1:4, *Notes*) that is "grown up to the measure of the stature of Christ; being full of his light, grace, wisdom [and] holiness" (Colossians 4:12, *Notes*). It shuns sin and embraces what is true and right. It is filled with the fullness of God and loves God with all that we are and have. It loves others as we love ourselves. Holiness of heart and life is the way of happiness and joy. Holiness is the path of blessing in this life and in the next (2 Peter 3:18, *Notes*).

ASSESSMENT

What can we say regarding the value of Wesley's *Explanatory Notes Upon the New Testament* as doctrinal standards for The United Methodist Church? They are certainly an important link to our history, since they have long been considered an expression of Wesleyan thought. But what worth do they have for us? Despite the reasons cited early in this chapter for why the *Notes* are not widely used, they provide three significant lessons that continue to instruct United Methodists.

First, the *Notes* show that Wesley knew the Bible to be the most important book that Christians possess. It is the principal place where we not only discover the God who creates the universe and everything in it but the same God who cares for creation and, more especially, loves everyone in it. Wesley spoke of himself as *homo unius libri*, a man of one book, and urged the Methodist people, lay and clergy, to follow him in a commitment to its authority. They were to read, study, and put into practice the biblical message. Wesley's commentaries on the Old and New Testaments were intended to help them understand and appreciate the Bible's words and ideas. He would be puzzled and deeply disappointed with the biblical illiteracy of United Methodists today. There is little doubt that a fresh reading of the New Testament *Notes* with other aids to biblical study would enrich our knowledge of and respect for the Bible. That was Wesley's intention.

Second, Wesley identified the major themes of Christian faith in the *Notes*. We have described them as (1) the human situation apart from God, (2) the saving work of God, and (3) the Christian life of holiness. We have pointed out that the *Notes* do not contain a detailed and complete system of Christian doctrine, but Wesley felt they embodied the core of Christian beliefs. Among these beliefs are a recognition of the seriousness of the sinful condition in which we live; the initiative of the grace of the triune God in forgiving us and granting us a new beginning; the centrality of the life, atoning death, and resurrection of Jesus; and the grand opportunity of a disciplined Christian life lived with God's blessing, using God's gifts and serving God through engaging in worship and ministry (through works of piety and works of mercy). Wesley believed that we should guard these basic concepts with unflagging courage and commitment.

Third, the *Notes* illuminate perhaps the fundamental concept of Christianity that seems most critical in our time: our understanding of the person and work of Christ. In the discipline of Christian theology, this is called *Christology*. It deals with such questions as "Who is Jesus?" "What is his significance?" "What is the meaning of his life, death, and resurrection?" Wesley's *Notes* give clear answers to these questions. Throughout the *Notes*, Jesus is called God and identified as the second person of the Holy Trinity (for example, John 1:1-18; 14:11; Colossians 1:15-20; 1 John 5:20; Revelation 20:6, *Notes*). Affirming Jesus as God in no way denied his enfleshment (the Incarnation) during his earthly ministry. Jesus came in the flesh and was genuinely human (1 John 2:22, *Notes*). So, Wesley affirmed the traditional Christian view that in Jesus humanity and divinity resided equally. Wesley held that this was a mystery (Revelation 20:2, *Notes*), as we do. Furthermore, Jesus' death was sacrificial. Through it God did something for us we cannot do for ourselves. Through Christ, God forgives, redeems, reconciles, saves, and begins the process of new life in us, the goal of which is complete holiness of heart and life. Wesley was quite plain in saying that Christ is "our only wisdom, righteousness, [and] sanctification" (2 Corinthians 4:5, *Notes*). He *alone* is our Redeemer, and we have salvation only through him (Galatians 1:4, *Notes*).

There are, however, several places where Wesley's comments in the *Notes* contain inaccuracies or raise serious questions for United Methodists today. While it is difficult to locate many outright errors in the commentary, there are a few. For example, there is a very plain mistake in the comment on Mark 7:31-37, the account of a "deaf and dumb" man brought to Jesus to be healed. In his closing remarks on this passage, Wesley referred to the person healed as a "blind man." The scriptural text does not describe him as blind.

There are other areas where we might raise more serious questions about Wesley's interpretations. Among these are his comments on baptism, women, Roman Catholicism and the papacy, and eschatology (the doctrine of "last things"). In at least these four areas, our commitment to the Bible itself requires us to correct or to move beyond Wesley's views.

(a) Baptism
It has already been said that the *Notes* affirm the baptism of infants and adults as an important means by which God conveys saving grace into the life of the person baptized. The problem in the *Notes* is not so much with what baptism does, as with the mode by which it is administered. Wesley believed that baptism could be done by immersion, pouring, or sprinkling (Colossians 2:12, *Notes*). Any of these three ways of administering baptism is valid. This is the current position of The United

Methodist Church. However, Wesley's bias for sprinkling (and perhaps pouring) is clear. To support his own preference, he took considerable license in portraying John the Baptist splashing those he baptized rather than immersing them, when immersion was probably the manner in which John baptized (Matthew 3:6, *Notes*). Wesley allowed his own partiality for sprinkling to dictate his commentary on the biblical text.

(b) Women

The comments concerning women in the *Notes* are much more problematic than those on baptism. Wesley spoke of women having "less courage than men" (Acts 17:4, *Notes*). Women, he observed, are "naturally weak" and, therefore, to be treated with more tenderness than men (Hebrews 11:35; 1 Peter 3:7, *Notes*). Furthermore, it was not the place of women to speak in the congregation. It was man's role "to lead and to instruct the congregation" (1 Corinthians 14:34, *Notes*). Wesley, however, did provide an exception for women's addressing gatherings of the church if they were "under an extraordinary impulse of the Spirit" (1 Corinthians 14:34, *Notes*). On the other hand, he did affirm that male and female are one in Christ: "Neither is preferred before the other in [Christ's] kingdom" (1 Corinthians 11:11, *Notes*). Wesley also recognized the role of female deacons (deaconesses) to share in ministries to the poor (Acts 6:2, *Notes*) and delineated the office of deaconess in Romans 16:1. There he said that deaconesses were "not to teach publicly, but to visit the sick, . . . women in particular, and to minister to them both in their temporal and spiritual necessities" (Romans 16:1, *Notes*). Later in his ministry Wesley's views on women's role in the church changed significantly when he observed the important work women did in organizing and leading Methodist small group classes and preaching in the Methodist society meetings. Nevertheless, we will quarrel with some of his commentary regarding the capabilities, competence, and calling of women. God abundantly blesses the church through the presence, service, gifts, and leadership of women.

(c) Roman Catholicism and the Papacy

Wesley's views on the Roman Catholic Church and the papacy were products of his eighteenth-century environment. While his "Letter to a Roman Catholic," published in 1749, expressed an openness to Roman Catholics as brothers and sisters in the faith, the *Notes* reflect harsh criticism of Roman Catholicism, especially the papacy. Wesley identified the pope as "the man of sin" and "the son of perdition" (2 Thessalonians 2:3, *Notes*). Wesley's lengthy commentary on Revelation 13 set forth a view of history in which the papacy is referred to as the "antichrist" whose power has accomplished great evil over the centuries (Revelation 13:15, *Notes*) and continues to undermine Christ's kingdom. In this age of ecumenicity, even when we acknowledge some of the major differences between Roman Catholicism and Protestantism, we find it difficult to approve the interpretation of the Roman Catholic Church and the papacy set forth in the *Notes*.

(d) Eschatology (the doctrine of last things)

Wesley was a student of history as well as a biblical scholar. He combined his understanding of historical incidents with biblical events and ideas, especially in his interpretation of the Book of Revelation. Although in his introductory comments to Revelation he wrote, "I by no means pretend to understand or explain all that is contained in this mysterious book" (*Notes*), like other commentators he could not resist publishing a scheme that speculated on the course of history and progress toward the end of time. At the end of his commentary on Revelation, he produced a chronological timeline, which he called "a short view of the whole contents" (*Notes*) of the book, which involved a complicated correlation of texts from Revelation with various historical events through the centuries since it was written. He was reluctant to give a precise date for the end of the world, but he was convinced that something important would occur in 1836 when events described in Revelation 19 and 20 would be fulfilled. 1836 would be several years after his own death in 1791. It now appears that 1836 was not a significant year in God's plan of bringing history to its completion.

In these four illustrations—baptism, women, Roman Catholicism and the papacy, and eschatology—we are reminded that some of Wesley's comments simply cannot be used today as a guide for our belief and life. Changing historical circumstances and new insights in interpreting the Bible lead us into ways of thinking that differ from Wesley. We will, therefore, find it difficult to accept some of his commentary as binding for our understanding, preaching, teaching, and practice of the Christian faith.

CONCLUSION

Wesley's *Explanatory Notes Upon the New Testament* are the most neglected of the doctrinal standards of The United Methodist Church. In spite of some obvious limitations and flaws, they are one of the most important historical documents in our history. More significantly, they lay out what we consider to be the heart of the Christian faith in a plain and direct manner. They make clear our desperate situation apart from God, God's saving work on our behalf, and our response to God in the holy life. Read and studied in context with Wesley's Standard Sermons, the Methodist Articles of Religion, and the Evangelical United Brethren Confession of Faith, the *Explanatory Notes Upon the New Testament* remain the "traditional standard exposition of distinctive Methodist teaching" (*Book of Discipline*; Para. 61).

Some Questions for Reflection and Discussion

(1) John Wesley's *Explanatory Notes Upon the New Testament* are one of the doctrinal standards of The United Methodist Church. Had you ever seen or heard about them before reading this chapter? Secure a printed copy of the *Notes*, or use the website listed on the next page to view them.

(2) Wesley spoke about his commitment to be a person whose faith was rooted in the Bible and the necessity of his people being "Bible-Christians." What does the Bible mean to you? What is its importance in your life? Do you have a plan for reading and studying the Bible? What resources do you use to understand it?

(3) What are the stumbling blocks in your life that are evidence of rebellion against God and the mistreatment and neglect of your neighbors?

(4) The *Notes* make plain that salvation is the work of the triune God. We speak and sing about the Trinity (one God in three persons) in our worship. Have you thought about God in this way? Does it make sense to you?

(5) What is the significance of Jesus for your faith? What does it mean to speak about him as "prophet, priest, and king"? Is this a helpful way to think about Jesus? How do you react to the statement that Jesus is the *only* Redeemer and Savior of the world?

(6) Who is the Holy Spirit? Have you experienced the Spirit's presence in your life? If so, how? What gifts of the Holy Spirit do you possess, and in what ways do you use them?

(7) What do you think about Wesley's views on money?

(8) Wesley believed that we need to pay attention to the hindrances to holiness in our lives. What are these hindrances for you?

SUGGESTIONS FOR FURTHER READING AND STUDY

Jones, Scott J. *John Wesley's Conception and Use of Scripture*. Nashville: Abingdon Press, 1995. Examines what Wesley said about Scripture and analyzes how he interpreted and used it.

Wesley, John. *Explanatory Notes Upon the New Testament*. London: The Epworth Press, 1954. This is a reprint of the original edition.

_____. *Explanatory Notes Upon the New Testament*. 2 vols. Kansas City, MO: Beacon Hill Press of Kansas City, 1983. This is a reprint of the *Notes* from an undated earlier edition.

_____. *Explanatory Notes Upon the New Testament*. Available on the World Wide Web at http://wesley.nnu.edu. This web site offers the complete text of the New Testament *Notes* as well as the complete text of Wesley's Old Testament *Notes*.

---

[1] All quotations from *Notes*, unless otherwise indicated, are from *Explanatory Notes Upon the New Testament*, by John Wesley (Beacon Hill Press, 1983).

[2] From the "Model Deed," in *A History of The Methodist Church in Great Britain*, Vol. 4 (Epworth Press, 1988); page 151.

[3] From Letter to John Smith, September 28, 1745, in *The Works of John Wesley*, Vol. 26, edited by Frank Baker (Oxford University Press, 1982); page 155.

[4] All quotations from *Works*, unless otherwise indicated, are from *The Works of John Wesley*, Vols. 1–4, edited by Albert C. Outler (Abingdon Press, 1984–1987).

[5] From Preface, *Explanatory Notes Upon the Old Testament*, by John Wesley (Schmul Publishers, 1975).

[6] From Preface, *Explanatory Notes Upon the Old Testament*.

[7] All quotations from *The United Methodist Hymnal*, unless otherwise indicated, are from *The United Methodist Hymnal* (Copyright © 1989 The United Methodist Publishing House).

[8] From *The Poetical Works of John and Charles Wesley*, Vol. 1., collected and arranged by G. Osborn (1868); pp. 88–89.

CHAPTER 2
THE STANDARD SERMONS OF
JOHN WESLEY

From its earliest days, Methodism has been known for its preaching. Lay preachers were a significant force in the extension of the Methodist movement. Ordained clergy proclaimed the good news with vigor and enthusiasm. They followed the path pioneered by Methodism's founder, John Wesley, whose preaching, while not as dramatic as some, was an effective means for declaring the gospel, inviting response, and bringing people into the Methodist fold.

Wesley's published journal is adequate testimony to his devotion to preaching. Based on his journal entries and other information, it is estimated that he preached 40,000 sermons during the course of his ministry. In addition to the sermons he delivered orally, he also prepared 151 sermons for publication. All of them are available in the first four volumes of the Bicentennial Edition of *The Works of John Wesley*, edited by Albert C. Outler.[1] They are the second doctrinal standard of The United Methodist Church we will consider.

HISTORICAL BACKGROUND

In the first edition of the collected sermons that Wesley published (1746), he included a Preface in which he stated several important purposes for which these sermons were circulated. First, he said, they contained the substance of what he had been preaching and teaching for the last few years. Anyone who read and studied them would clearly understand the doctrines he embraced and taught "as the essentials of true religion" (*Works*; Vol. 1, page 103).

Second, they were intended to be a plain statement of the Christian faith for the general public. "I design plain truth for plain people" (Preface, *Works*; Vol. 1, page 104), he claimed. He continued:

Therefore of set purpose I abstain from all nice and philosophical speculations; from all perplexed and intricate reasonings, and as far as possible from even the show of learning, unless in sometimes citing the original Scriptures. I labour to avoid all words which are not easy to be understood, all which are not used in common life; and in particular those kinds of technical terms that so frequently occur in bodies of divinity, those modes of speaking which [people] of reading are intimately acquainted with, but which to common people are an unknown tongue. (Preface, *Works*; Vol. 1, page 104)

Wesley was more specific about the audience for whom the published sermons were intended. He designed them especially for two groups of people. The first were new Christians who were "just setting their faces toward heaven" who had "little acquaintance with the things of God" (Preface, *Works*; Vol.1, page 106). They needed the encouragement and instruction that the sermons would provide. The second were those already well established in the faith, who had adopted "the religion of the heart, the faith which worketh by love" (Preface, *Works*; Vol. 1, page 106) but who always faced the prospect of falling away from the way of Christ. They required the support and exhortation that the sermons embodied.

Third, Wesley believed that his sermons were thoroughly grounded in the Bible. He asserted that in writing the sermons, he had put aside all that he had ever read except the Scripture in order to be "homo unius libri" (a man of one book) (Preface, *Works*; Vol. 1, page 105). "O give me that book!" he wrote. "At any price give me the Book of God! I have it. Here is knowledge enough for me" (Preface, *Works*; Vol. 1, page 105). "I want to know one thing, the way to heaven," he stated, "how to land safe on that happy shore" (Preface, *Works*; Vol. 1, page 105). The Bible teaches us that way.

Fourth, Wesley was aware that some of the views expressed in his sermons were disputed. Not everyone agreed with all he had to say. To his critics he said that if he had mistaken the path of truth, he was ready to learn where he had gone astray and to be corrected. But the correction had to be based on the Bible. "Point me out a better way than I have yet known. Show me it is so by plain proof of Scripture" (Preface, *Works*; Vol.1, page 107). At the very least, he begged, he and those who differed with him on theological matters must not provoke one another to anger but love each other. "For how far is love, even with many wrong opinions, to be preferred before truth itself without love?" (Preface, *Works*; Vol. 1, page 107), he wrote. Wesley was not arguing here for "wrong opinions"; he was reminding Christians that under all circumstances love must be uppermost.

Wesley published the first collection of some of his sermons in 1746. As the Methodist movement grew, he decided to bring together more sermon collections. By 1761, there were four volumes of his sermons in print containing forty-three sermons. In 1763, when Wesley drew up the "Model Deed," mentioned in the previous chapter, he specified that only those persons were permitted to preach in Methodist buildings who preached "no other Doctrine than is contained in Mr. W's *Notes Upon the New Testament* and four volumes of *Sermons.*"[2] So, Wesley's sermons had an important role in the life and thought of the Methodist people.

In 1788, Wesley published a new collection of his sermons that included one hundred sermons in eight volumes. This was the last collection issued during his lifetime. The Bicentennial Edition of *The Works of John Wesley* includes four volumes of sermons and includes not only the sermon collections he published but also other sermons written by him that were printed in Methodist publications before and after his death. There are 151 sermons in these volumes (The last sermon is a Latin version of the one that precedes it.). *The Book of Discipline of The United Methodist Church* identifies the sermons in the Bicentennial Edition as "The Standard Sermons of Wesley" and, therefore, doctrinal standards for the denomination.

CONTENT

It may be more difficult to set forth the main ideas of the sermons than the main ideas of the *Explanatory Notes Upon the New Testament*, since the sermons deal in more detail with a wider range of topics. Yet the sermons and *Notes* contain some of the same emphases. The following seem to be seven primary themes. Where there are quotes from the sermons, the sermon title is identified in the parentheses.

(1) Original Sin

What is the major problem with human beings and the human community? John Wesley was not at a loss to declare what is at the root of all our difficulties. It is wickedness and sin. It manifests itself in our relationships with God and with our neighbors. In Wesley's words the sinful state is:

Against God: forgetfulness and contempt of God, of his name, his day [the sabbath], his Word, his ordinances [sacraments]; [it is] atheism on the one hand and idolatry on the other; in particular, love of the world, the desire of the flesh, the desire of the eyes, and the pride of life; the love of money, the love of power, the love of ease, the love of the 'honor that cometh of men', the love of the creature more than the Creator, . . . being lovers of pleasure more than lovers of God. Against our neighbour: [it is] ingratitude, revenge, hatred, envy, malice, uncharitableness. ("The Deceitfulness of the Human Heart," *Works*; Vol. 4, page 156)

Sin accounts for the great chasm that exists between what God intends us to be and what we really are. Every one of us lives in this sinful state. Each of us is flawed and "imperfect" ("Of Evil Angels," *Works*; Vol. 3, page 16). Wesley described sin's serious effect on us: "Our body, soul, and spirit, are infected, overspread, consumed, with the most fatal leprosy. We are all over, within and without, in the eye of God, full of diseases, and wounds, and putrifying sores" ("The One Thing Needful," *Works*; Vol. 4, page 354). Our situation is desperate, even though we may not be aware of the danger.

Wesley believed that sin had its origin in the parents of the human race, Adam and Eve, and their fall. Their unbelief, "independence, self-will, and pride" ("The Deceitfulness of the Human Heart," *Works*; Vol. 4, page 154) produced in them ungodliness and unrighteousness. Wesley explained:

When Satan had once transfused his own self-will and pride into the parents of mankind, together with a new species of sin—love of the world, the loving the creature above the Creator—all manner of wickedness soon rushed in, all ungodliness and unrighteousness, shooting out into crimes of every kind, soon covering the whole face of the earth with all manner of abominations. It would be an endless task to enumerate all the enormities [of sin] that broke out. ("The Deceitfulness of the Human Heart," *Works*; Vol. 4, page 152)

Wesley was convinced that Adam's sin was transmitted to all humanity from one generation to another, although he confessed that he did not understand how this happens. In a lengthy book titled *The Doctrine of Original Sin*, published in 1756, Wesley wrote, "If you ask me, how, in what determinate manner, sin is propagated; how it is transmitted from father to son: I answer plainly, I cannot tell."[3]

The consequences of sin are awful. Sin turns us away from God and the blessings we are intended to enjoy. It turns us away from our neighbors and the harmony we are meant to experience with others. It produces chaos, guilt, unhappiness, and fear in us. Its most dire result is that it leads us to "everlasting destruction" and "banishment from the presence of the Lord" ("Of Hell," *Works*; Vol. 3, page 35). Although he was not preoccupied with the notion of eternal punishment of the wicked, Wesley was persuaded that it was taught in Scripture and to be feared by the sinner.

In a poignant hymn Charles Wesley spoke about the serious condition and need of sinners:

> Wretched, helpless, and distressed,
>   Ah! Whither shall I fly?
> Ever grasping after rest,
>   I cannot find it nigh;
> Naked, sick, and poor, and blind,
>   Fast bound in sin and misery,
> Friend of sinners, let me find
>   My help, my all in thee!
>
> I am all unclean, unclean,
>   Thy purity I want;
> My whole heart is sick of sin,
>   And my whole head is faint!
> Full of putrifying sores,
> Of bruises, and of wounds, my soul
> Looks to Jesus, help implores,
>   And gasps to be made whole.
>
> In the wilderness I stray,
>   My foolish heart is blind;
> Nothing do I know; the way
>   Of peace I cannot find;
> Jesu, Lord, restore my sight,
> And take, O take the veil away,
> Turn my darkness into light,
>   My midnight into day.
>
> Naked of thine image, Lord,
>   Forsaken, and alone,
> Unrenewed, and unrestored,
>   I have not thee put on.
> Over me thy mantle spread,
> Send down thy likeness from above,
> Let thy goodness be displayed,
>   And wrap me in thy love!
>   (*A Collection of Hymns;* 105)

Who will save us from the judgment and punishment we deserve? Who will heal us of our disease and restore us to whole life? The answer to these crucial questions is God's grace, God's unearned, undeserved, unmerited love.

(2) Prevenient Grace

Prevenient grace is identified as one of the "distinctive Wesleyan emphases" (*Book of Discipline*; Para. 60, pages 43–44). "Prevenient Grace" is also the title of a section of *The United Methodist Hymnal* (Hymns 338–59). Yet many United Methodists are unfamiliar with this term and its meaning.

John Wesley did not use the term *prevenient grace*. He employed the term *preventing grace* ("The Witness of the Spirit, II," *Works*; Vol. 1, page 298). Today we use the word *prevent* to mean to hinder or hold back. But the term can also mean, as Wesley used it, to go ahead of something or someone. It is this latter meaning that Wesley intended. "Preventing grace" and "prevenient grace" are synonymous. Prevenient grace is the divine love that surrounds all of us. It is the grace that goes before and prepares us for further expressions of God's love and purpose in our lives.

Prevenient, or preparing, grace is at work in all people through the presence of the Holy Spirit. It is "free in all, and free for all" ("Free Grace," *Works*; Vol. 3, page 544). Our salvation and healing begins, according to Wesley, with this grace that includes:

> the first wish to please God, the first dawn of light concerning his will, and the first slight, transient conviction of having sinned against him. All these imply some tendency toward life, some degree of salvation, the beginning of a deliverance from a blind, unfeeling heart, quite insensible of God and the things of God. ("On Working Out Our Own Salvation," *Works*; Vol. 3, pages 203–204)

God's preparing grace stirs us to acknowledge the lamentable sinful condition in which we live apart from God, leads us to the way of new life, makes it possible for us to respond to God's free offer of forgiveness and reconciliation, and moves us to repentance (a complete turning to God and the reorientation of our lives around God's presence and will).

While some say that human beings are not free because sin has destroyed their ability to respond to God, Wesley believed that *all* are liberated by God's prevenient grace to accept or reject the forgiveness, salvation, and healing God proffers. Wesley completely rejected any idea that assumed that God had determined before their birth who would be condemned and who would be granted new life. In his important sermon "Free Grace," Wesley stated a number of additional objections he had to this idea. He believed that this kind of "predestinarian" theology was unscriptural. It makes preaching worthless, since it holds that God has already chosen who is to be forgiven. It discourages holy living because once people believe they are elected by God for salvation and cannot lose it, they are not motivated to live a righteous life. Furthermore, it makes God worse than the devil, since it presents God seeking the salvation of all people while deliberately withholding saving grace from some of them. Wesley was convinced that by God's prevenient grace all are free.

Many of Charles Wesley's hymns reflect the idea of prevenient grace by inviting all people to accept God's reconciling love, thereby assuming that they are free to do so. Here is one:

> Come, sinners, to the gospel feast;
>   let *every* soul be Jesus' guest.
> Ye need not one be left behind,
>   for God hath bid *all* humankind.
>
> Sent by my Lord, on you I call;
>   the invitation is to *all*.
> Come, *all* the world! Come, sinner, thou!
>   All things in Christ are ready now.
>
> Come, *all* ye souls by sin oppressed,
>   ye restless wanderers after rest;
> ye poor, and maimed, and halt, and blind,
>   in Christ a hearty welcome find.
>
> My message as from God receive;
>   ye *all* may come to Christ and live.
> O let his love your hearts constrain,
>   nor suffer him to die in vain.
>
> This is the time, no more delay!
>   This is the Lord's accepted day.
> Come thou, this moment, at his call,
>   and live for him who died for *all*.
> (*The United Methodist Hymnal*; 339, emphasis added)

(3) Justification by Faith

God's prevenient grace prepares the way for God's justifying grace, the gift of divine forgiveness and reconciliation. A section of *The United Methodist Hymnal* (361–81) includes a series of hymns that celebrate justifying grace. United Methodists are one with other Christians in recognizing the importance of justification by faith, an idea that is deeply rooted in the Bible (for example, Romans 5:1-2; Galatians 3:24).

Wesley clearly defined justification. It is, he wrote, "another word for pardon. It is the forgiveness of all our sins, and . . . our acceptance with God" ("The Scripture Way of Salvation," *Works*; Vol. 2, page 157). It concerns how unrighteous people stand before the righteous God. They deserve nothing but God's judgment and wrath. It is impossible for them to justify themselves because they do not live the holy life that God requires. They do not deserve and cannot earn God's pardon. It is the gift of God that we receive through our trustful dependence on God's love.

Justification is the work of the triune God. This triune God justifies us and heals our soul's diseases. However, the second person of the Trinity, Jesus Christ, is the central figure in our justification. His life, death, and resurrection are crucial acts by which we are pardoned. As he did in his *Explanatory Notes Upon the New Testament*, Wesley described Jesus' three important titles: Prophet, Priest, and King. Jesus is the prophet, " 'who of God is made unto us wisdom', who by his word and Spirit 'is with us always', 'guiding us into all truth' " ("The Law Established Through Faith, II," *Works*; Vol. 2, pages 37–38). Charles Wesley spoke of Christ the prophet in the following hymn stanza:

> Prophet, to me reveal
> Thy Father's perfect will:
> Never mortal spake like thee,
> Human prophet like divine;
> Loud and strong their voices be,
> Small, and still, and inward thine!
> (*A Collection of Hymns*; 186)

Jesus the priest is " 'reconciling us to God by his blood', and 'ever living to make intercession for us' " ("The Law Established Through Faith, II," *Works*; Vol. 2, page 37). Jesus did something for us we cannot do for ourselves. His death was a perfect atoning sacrifice offered for us by which we are justified, reconciled with God, and receive God's healing forgiveness. Again, in Charles's words:

> Jesus, our great high priest,
> hath full atonement made;
> ye weary spirits rest;
> ye mournful souls be glad:
> . . . .

Extol the Lamb of God,
the all-atoning Lamb;
redemption in his blood
throughout the world
proclaim.
(*The United Methodist Hymnal*; 379)

Jesus is the king, "restoring those to the image of God whom he ... first reinstated in his favor; ... reigning in all believing hearts until he has 'subdued all things to himself'; until he hath utterly cast out all sin, and 'brought in everlasting righteousness.' " ("The Law Established Through Faith, II," *Works*; Vol. 2, page 38). In Charles's words,

Rejoice the Lord is King!
Your Lord and King adore;
mortals, give thanks and sing,
and triumph evermore.
Lift up your heart,
lift up your voice;
rejoice; again I say, rejoice.

Jesus the Savior reigns,
the God of truth and love;
when he had purged our stains,
he took his seat above.
Lift up your heart,
lift up your voice;
rejoice; again I say, rejoice.
(*The United Methodist Hymnal*; 715)

Justification by faith is rooted in God's accepting grace, pardoning, forgiving, reconciling, and redeeming us. Justifying grace lays the foundation for our renewal, transformation, and healing.

(4) New Birth
Justification by faith is accompanied by new birth. The two cannot be separated, although for purposes of discussing them, Wesley believed, they may be distinguished. Wesley wrote:

If any doctrines within the whole compass of Christianity may be properly termed fundamental they are doubtless these two—the doctrine of justification, and that of the new birth: the former relating to that great work which God does *for us*, in forgiving our sins; the latter to the great work which God does *in us*, in renewing our fallen nature. In order of time neither of these is before the other. In the moment we are justified by the grace of God through the redemption that is in Jesus we are also 'born of the Spirit'; but in order of thinking, as it is termed, justification precedes the new birth. We first conceive his wrath to be turned away, and then his Spirit to work in our hearts. ("The New Birth," *Works*; Vol. 2, page 187)

In the same sermon Wesley expanded his description of how he understood the new birth. He wrote:

It is that great change which God works in the soul when he brings it into life: when he raises it from the death of sin to the life of righteousness. It is the change wrought in the whole soul by the almighty Spirit of God when it is 'created anew in Christ Jesus', when it is 'renewed after the image of God', 'in righteousness and true holiness', when the love of the world is changed into the love of God, pride into humility, passion into meekness; hatred, envy, malice, into a sincere, tender, disinterested love for all mankind. In a word, it is that change whereby the 'earthly, sensual, devilish' mind is turned into 'the mind which was in Christ'. This is the nature of the new birth. 'So is everyone that is born of the Spirit.' ("The New Birth," *Works*; Vol. 2, pages 193–94)

The new birth points to the reality of grace actually changing us deep within ourselves. To make this clearer, Wesley compared spiritual new birth to the birth of a child. In the womb the unborn has eyes but cannot see, ears but cannot hear, and other undeveloped senses. After birth the child's senses are activated in a new fashion. Light, sound, and other sensory experiences occur. It is similar for new-born Christians. They enjoy new life. They see God's presence and love at work. They hear God's word of challenge and comfort. Their spiritual senses are energized. They are prepared for the new life in which God wants them to take pleasure. (See "The New Birth," *Works*; Vol. 2 and "The Great Privilege of Those That Are Born of God," *Works*; Vol. 1.)

There are at least three scriptural marks of this new birth: faith, hope, and love. People born of God possess *faith*, "a sure trust and confidence in God that through the merits of Christ" ("The Marks of the New Birth,"

Works; Vol. 1, page 418) they are forgiven and reconciled to God and free from the dominating power of sin. They have *hope*, rejoicing in the presence of the Holy Spirit who assures them of the truth and blessings of God's promises. "A third scriptural mark of those who are born of God," wrote Wesley, "and the greatest of all, is *love*: even the 'love of God shed abroad in their hearts by the Holy Ghost which is given unto them'" ("The Marks of the New Birth," *Works*; Vol. 1, page 425). The love about which Wesley spoke has two dimensions. It is, first of all, love for God. This includes focusing life on God, accepting the gifts God gives, worshiping and serving God with all we are and have. Second, it means loving our neighbor:

> The necessary fruit of [the] love of God is the love of our neighbour, of every soul which God hath made; not excepting our enemies, not excepting those who are now 'despitefully using and persecuting us'; a love whereby we love every man *as ourselves*—as we love our own souls. Nay, our Lord has expressed it still more strongly, teaching us to 'love one another even as he hath loved us'. ("The Marks of the New Birth," *Works*; Vol. 1, page 426)

Many hymns of Charles Wesley celebrate the experience of the changed life that the new birth inaugurates. Stanzas from two of these hymns illustrate this idea:

> There for me the Savior stands,
> shows his wounds and
> spreads his hands.
> God is love! I know, I *feel*;
> Jesus weeps and loves me
> still.
> (*The United Methodist Hymnal*; 355, emphasis added)

> Long my imprisoned spirit lay,
> fast bound in sin and
> nature's night;
> thine eye diffused a quickening
> ray;
> I woke, the dungeon flamed
> with light;
> my chains fell off, my heart was
> free,

I rose, went forth, and
followed thee.
(*The United Methodist Hymnal*; 363)

(5) Assurance

We should know whose children we are. Are we children of God or children of the devil? Wesley was sure that the children of God should know who they are and whose they are. They are recipients of God's prevenient (preparing) and justifying (accepting) grace. They have been inwardly changed, born anew, and set on a new path by the triune God. This is a reality we accept with humility and thanksgiving. Furthermore, the Bible teaches and Christian experience confirms that the Holy Spirit, the third person of the Trinity, bears witness that we have a secure standing with God. Referring especially to Romans 8:16, Wesley called this the "witness" or "testimony of the Holy Spirit." He explained:

> The testimony of the [Holy] Spirit is an inward impression on the soul, whereby the Spirit of God directly 'witnesses to my spirit that I am a child of God'; that Jesus Christ hath loved me, and given himself for me; that all my sins are blotted out, and I, even I, am reconciled to God. ("The Witness of the Spirit, I," *Works*; Vol. 1, page 274)

Wesley was at a loss to explain the way in which the Spirit accomplished this work in the life of the believer. It is another of God's mysteries. He wrote:

> I do not mean . . . that the Spirit of God testifies this by an outward voice; no, nor always by an inward voice, although he may do this sometimes. Neither do I suppose that he always applies to the heart (though he often may) one or more texts of scripture. But he so works upon the soul by his immediate influence, and by a strong though inexplicable operation, that the stormy wind and troubled waves subside, and there is a sweet calm; the heart resting as in the arms of Jesus, and the sinner being clearly satisfied that God is reconciled, that all his 'iniquities are forgiven, and his sins covered'. ("The Witness of the Spirit, II," *Works*; Vol. 1, page 287)

Two of Charles Wesley's hymns speak of the assurance about which his brother wrote:

No condemnation now I dread;
   Jesus, and all in him, is
      mine;
alive in him, my living Head,
   and clothed in righteousness
      divine,
bold I approach th'eternal throne,
   and claim the crown,
      through Christ my own.
(*The United Methodist Hymnal*; 363)

Inspire the living faith
   (which whosoe'er receive,
the witness in themselves they
      have
   and consciously believe),
the faith that conquers all,
   and doth the mountain
      move,
and saves whoe'er on Jesus call,
and perfects them in love.
(*The United Methodist Hymnal*; 332)

The Holy Spirit brings gifts that nurture the life of the believer and strengthen the body of Christ. The Spirit also produces "fruit" in us. "If the Spirit of God does really testify that we are children of God, the immediate consequence will be the fruit of the Spirit, even 'love, joy, peace, long-suffering, gentleness, goodness, fidelity, meekness, temperance'," wrote Wesley ("The Witness of the Spirit, I," *Works*; Vol. 1, page 297).

(6) Holiness of Heart and Life

Holiness is one of the most important terms in the Wesleyan vocabulary. It has its roots in the Bible. The term *holy* is an important biblical word. It appears frequently in both the Old Testament and the New Testament. God is described as the Holy One of Israel (1 Samuel 2:2; Psalms 78:41; 89:18). The holy God is completely different from the rest of creation. God's being and presence create a sense of wonder and awe in us. Furthermore, when people accept God's forgiving grace and accept the divine invitation to live focused on God, they become a holy people and live holy lives by God's grace using God's gifts. Another important biblical term, akin to holiness, is *sanctification* (Romans 6:22; 1 Corinthians 1:30; 1 Thessalonians 4:3). Holiness and sanctification represent concepts that are prominent in the writings of John Wesley, including his sermons.

Wesley understood holiness to be the aim of Christians. He was devoted to holy living throughout his life. He first learned about it from his parents. Then, as a young man, his study of the Bible and the great devotional writers of the church confirmed that Christians must be committed to holiness. By God's grace, holy living must be what they most seek to practice. At one place in his writings, Wesley underscored the importance of holiness by comparing the Christian faith to a house. The porch of the house is repentance (made possible by prevenient, preparing grace). The door of the house is justification by faith (God's pardoning, forgiving, reconciling, accepting, renewing grace). The main structure of the house, however, for which the porch and door are means of access, is holiness of heart and life.[4]

Reflecting on the birth of Methodism among the students at Oxford University, Wesley observed that God raised them up

> to testify those grand truths which were then little attended to:
> That without holiness no man shall see the Lord;
> That this holiness is the work of God, who worketh in us both to will and to do;
> That he doeth it of his own good pleasure, merely for the merits of Christ;
> That this holiness is the mind that was in Christ, enabling us to walk as he also walked;
> That no man can be thus sanctified till he be justified; and
> That we are justified by faith alone. ("The General Spread of the Gospel," *Works*; Vol. 2, pages 490–91)

What is holiness? It consists of two dimensions: inward and outward holiness. Although these two dimensions are inseparable, we need to describe each of them individually. Inward holiness is being "singly fixed upon God" ("On a Single Eye," *Works*; Vol. 4, page 121) so that nothing else matters more than pleasing God in what we think, say, and do. "For whenever we are not aiming at God we are seeking happiness in some creature" ("On a Single Eye," *Works*; Vol. 4, page 123), Wesley wrote. To be holy is to believe in, trust, love, worship, imitate, and obey God. It means delighting in God, rejoicing in God's will, seeking and finding our happiness in God, and desiring fuller enjoyment of God ("On Love," *Works*; Vol. 4, page 383). It is to rely on God's sustaining grace in order to become what God intends us to be. Wesley was fully persuaded that such holiness is not produced by human effort. Only God can make us holy through the presence of the Holy Spirit and the utilization of God's gifts. Of the many gifts God gives for deepening our holiness, there are a few that Wesley thought to be especially helpful. They are searching the Scriptures, prayer, fasting, Christian conference, and the Lord's Supper. We need to say something about each of these gifts that Wesley referred to as "means of grace" ("The Means of Grace," *Works*; Vol. 1, page 381). When employed by faithful people, he also called them "works of piety" ("The Sermon on the Mount, VI," *Works*; Vol. 1, page 575).

(a) Searching the Scriptures

We noted in the last chapter how important the Bible was for Wesley. His writings, including all his sermons, are saturated with biblical quotations. In the Preface to the publication of his collected sermons, we encounter again his claim that he was devoutly "a man of one book." "Let me be *homo unius libri*" (Preface, *Works*; Vol. 1, page 105), he wrote. We repeat the observation that Wesley was a man of many books. He constantly read many different subjects,such as geography; science; history; philosophy; and, of course, theology. But of all the books available to him, and to us, he was convinced that the Bible is in a class of its own. It is absolutely indispensable for persons who desire to mature in holiness.

Searching the Scriptures means "hearing, reading, and meditating [on]" the biblical text regularly with the intention of meeting the triune God in the biblical word ("The Means of Grace," *Works*; Vol. 1, page 387). We take up the Scriptures individually or in the company of other Christians. We not only read the Bible for personal inspiration and direction, but we hear it read in corporate worship where it is used as a basis for preaching and teaching. Since the biblical message forms the basis for so many of the hymns we sing, especially Wesleyan hymns, our reading and hearing often involves our singing the Scriptures. Reading, hearing, and singing the biblical text are ways in which the Scriptures are introduced to our lives and to the life of the church.

The Wesleys were certain that we should seek the aid of God when we search the Scriptures. Charles offered a prayer-hymn that voices this sentiment:

> Come, divine Interpreter,
> bring me eyes thy book to
> read,
> ears the mystic words to hear,
> words which did from thee
> proceed,

words that endless bliss impart,
kept in an obedient heart.

All who read, or hear, are blessed,
if thy plain commands we do;
of thy kingdom here possessed,
thee we shall in glory view
when thou comest on earth to
      abide,
reign triumphant at thy side.
(*The United Methodist Hymnal*; 594)

(b) Prayer

Christians must employ the gift of prayer if they are to be the holy people God wants them to be. Prayer, for Wesley, was the major way in which we draw near to God; the absence of prayer in the life of a Christian cannot be replaced by anything else. Wesley wrote, "Nothing can be more plain than that the life of God in the soul does not continue, much less increase, unless we use all opportunities of communing with God, and pouring out our hearts before him" ("The Wilderness State," *Works*; Vol. 2, page 209). The neglect of prayer, both privately and corporately with others, primarily in worship, is a sin of omission and results in loss of faith, love, joy, peace, and power over sin.

Wesley's urging people to pray came out of his own experience of the importance of prayer. His journals and diaries show that he engaged in private prayer daily and discovered strength in it. But praying in private was not enough. He was always suspicious of a purely private religion. Therefore, Wesley also regularly joined others in morning and evening prayerful worship in parish churches and cathedrals, in Methodist societies and class meetings, and urged his followers to do the same.

Convinced that prayer is both a gift of God and an obligation for Christians, Wesley offered advice on praying out of his own practice. He advised that there are times when it is appropriate to make up our own prayers as led by the Holy Spirit. To sustain a vital lifetime of effective praying, however, it is wise to consider the vast riches of the church's devotional literature and prayerbooks. In keeping with this advice, Wesley published a few collections of prayers for the use of his followers, including *Prayers for Children* (1772).

Like many other Christians, Methodists have not simply *said* their prayers, they have also *sung* them. Our hymnals are full of the prayers we offer to God in poetry and music. Among them are many beautiful prayer-hymns written by Charles Wesley, including the following trinitarian text:

Maker, in whom we live,
    in whom we are and move,
the glory, power, and praise receive
    for thy creating love.
Let all the angel throng
    give thanks to God on high,
while earth repeats the joyful song
    and echoes to the sky.

Incarnate Deity, let all the ransomed race
    render in thanks their lives to thee for thy
        redeeming grace.
The grace to sinners showed ye heavenly choirs
    proclaim,
    and cry, "Salvation to our God,
        salvation to the Lamb."

Spirit of Holiness, let all thy saints adore
    thy sacred energy, and bless thine heart-
        renewing power.
Not angel tongues can tell thy love's ecstatic
    height,
    the glorious joy unspeakable, the beatific
    sight.

Eternal, Triune God, let all the hosts above,
    let all on earth below record and dwell
        upon thy love.
When heaven and earth are fled before thy
    glorious face,
    sing all the saints thy love hath made thine
    everlasting praise.
    (*The United Methodist Hymnal;* 88)

(c) Fasting

Among the "works of piety" necessary for holiness (sanctification) is fasting, abstaining from food. Wesley mentioned fasting positively in several of his sermons. One sermon, however, in his series on the Sermon on the Mount, was entirely devoted to it. He believed that fasting was well grounded in the Bible. It was practiced by people of Old Testament times, by Jesus, and by the earliest Christians. He saw no reason why it should be neglected by him or by other believers, mostly because he was persuaded that fasting advances holiness.

While there was precedence for fasting in Israel, in the commands of Jesus (Matthew 6:16-17), and in the early Christian community, there are other reasons for its performance. It is an expression of our repentance, especially for sins of excessive eating, drinking, or otherwise being immoderate by indulging "sensual appetites" ("Sermon on the Mount, VII," *Works*; Vol. 1, page 599). Fasting also allows us more time for study, prayer, and meditation. Furthermore, the money saved by fasting may be given to the poor so that they may have food and other necessities of life. As much as possible, fasting should be combined with doing good to others.

Wesley described the manner in which fasting was to be done. He wrote:

> Let it be done *unto the Lord*, with our eye singly fixed on him. Let our intention herein be this, and this alone, to glorify our Father which is in heaven; to express our sorrow and shame for our manifold transgressions of his holy law; to wait for an increase of purifying grace, drawing our affections to things above; to add seriousness and earnestness to our prayers; to avert the wrath of God, and to obtain all the great and precious promises which he hath made to us in Christ Jesus. ("Sermon on the Mount, VII," *Works*; Vol. 1, page 608)

A student of church history, Wesley was also aware that fasting had sometimes been carried to extremes. He observed, "Of all the means of grace there is scarce any concerning which men have run into greater extremes than . . . religious fasting. How have some exalted this beyond all Scripture and reason!" ("The Sermon on the Mount, VII," *Works*; Vol. 1, page 593). Fasting must never be undertaken to the point of jeopardizing one's health. He also advised against it when people are sick or otherwise unable.

A hymn by Charles Wesley speaks of the importance of prayer and fasting:

> With fasting and prayer My Saviour I seek,
> And listen to hear The Comforter speak:
> In searching and hearing The life-giving word,
> I wait Thy appearing, I look for my Lord.[5]

(d) Christian Community

Wesley was convinced that we cannot be Christians in solitude. Biblical religion is personal, but it is never private. If people are to be holy in heart and life, they need to give and receive the support, encouragement, and assistance of their sisters and brothers in Christ. They will experience this in public worship, study, and in ministry to others. For this reason Wesley formed societies and classes (small groups in each Methodist society) to meet weekly as a means by which God's grace would provide "spiritual helps" for his people ("On God's Vineyard," *Works*; Vol. 3, pages 502–17). In this Christian community Methodist people would minister to one another, withstand the temptations and assaults of evil, and work together to change society.

The quality of Christian community that Wesley envisioned was of the best sort. For example, when Christians gather to talk with one another, Wesley advised that their conversation should be appropriate to their calling in Christ. It should contain nothing "profane, nothing immodest, nothing untrue, or unkind"; and there should be "no talebearing, backbiting, or evil-speaking" among God's people ("The More Excellent Way," *Works*; Vol. 3, page 271).

Many of Charles Wesley's hymns speak of the deep relationships with one another that are characteristic of people genuinely committed to Christ.

> All praise to our redeeming Lord,
>   who joins us by his grace,
> and bids us, each to each
>   restored,
>   together seek his face.
>
> He bids us build each other up;
>   and, gathered into one,
> to our high calling's glorious hope
>   we hand in hand go on.
>
> The gift which he on one bestows,
>   we all delight to prove,
> the grace through every vessel
>   flows
>   in purest streams of love.
>
> E'en now we think and speak the
>   same,
>   and cordially agree,

concentered all, through Jesus'
    name,
in perfect harmony.

We all partake the joy of one;
    the common peace we feel,
a peace to sensual minds
    unknown,
a joy unspeakable.

And if our fellowship below
    in Jesus be so sweet,
what height of rapture
    shall we know when round
    his throne we meet!
(*The United Methodist Hymnal*; 554)

(e) Lord's Supper

As important as any of the "means of grace" or "works of piety" for
Wesley was the Lord's Supper, or Holy Communion. It is, Wesley wrote,
"the food of our souls" ("The Duty of Constant Communion," *Works*; Vol.
3, page 429). It was so important to him that he received it every three-to-
five days during his adult life.

There are two reasons why it was Wesley's practice regularly to receive
the Lord's Supper. First, it was the plain command of Jesus that his followers commune as often as possible. When Jesus said, "Do this in
remembrance of me" (Luke 22:19; 1 Corinthians 11:24), he was exhorting
his disciples to repeat regularly the sharing of bread and the cup. So, we
should obey Jesus' directions. Second, the benefits of those who keep
Jesus' commands include confirmation of the forgiveness of our sins and
the "strengthening and refreshing of our souls" ("The Duty of Constant
Communion," *Works*; Vol. 3, page 429). "All who desire an increase of the
grace of God are to wait for it in partaking of the Lord's Supper" ("The
Means of Grace," *Works*; Vol. 1, page 389), Wesley wrote.

While Wesley did not believe that the bread and wine become the actual
body and blood of Jesus (which is called "transubstantiation"), it is plain
that the Lord's Supper for Wesley was much more than a memorial meal
in which the recipients receive the bread and cup remembering what God
does for them. Wesley held that the bread and cup actually convey the
replenishing, sustaining grace of God when received by those who
believe and trust God for new life. He found it difficult to conceive of any
Christian whose maturity in holiness could occur without constantly

receiving God's grace in the Lord's Supper. It is the indispensable "food of our souls" ("The Duty of Constant Communion," *Works*; Vol. 3, page 429).

In 1745, John and Charles Wesley published a collection titled *Hymns on the Lord's Supper*. It contained an important theological section, based on the writing of Daniel Brevint, and 166 hymns. One of them reads:

> Jesu, my Lord and God, bestow
> All which Thy sacrament doth show,
> And make the real sign
> A sure effectual means of grace,
> Then sanctify my heart, and bless,
> And make it all like Thine.
>
> Great is thy faithfulness and love,
> Thine ordinance can never prove
> Of none effect, and vain;
> Only do Thou my heart prepare
> To findThy real presence there,
> And all Thy fulness gain.
> (*Hymns on the Lord's Supper*; 48)
>
> Come, Holy Ghost, Thine influence shed,
> And realize the sign;
> Thy life infuse into the bread,
> Thy power into the wine.
>
> Effectual let the tokens prove,
> And made, by heavenly art,
> Fit channels to convey Thy love
> To every faithful heart.
> (*Hymns on the Lord's Supper*; 51)

The first dimension of holiness, therefore, *inward holiness*, includes our personal commitment to live focused on God and centered on God's will for us. We do not stand alone in this. We are assisted by God's Spirit and gifts, including the support of other Christians in the church.

We turn now to a second dimension of holiness, recognizing that it is inseparable from the first. *Outward holiness* indicates Wesley's conviction that the holy life is demonstrated by the way in which we live with our families and communities. He wrote, "Christianity is essentially a social religion, and . . . to turn it into a solitary one is indeed to destroy it" ("Sermon on the Mount, IV," *Works*; Vol. 1, page 533). While there are times when we need to be by ourselves for thoughtful prayer and renewal, we cannot entirely separate ourselves from others. We are called into a world of great need. It is, Wesley wrote, "impossible ... to keep our religion from being seen, unless we cast it away. . . . Sure it is that a secret, unobserved religion cannot be the religion of Jesus Christ. Whatever religion can be concealed is not Christianity" ("Sermon on the Mount, IV," *Works*; Vol. 1, page 540). We show our love for God in our trust and obedience, in our worship, and in our love for our neighbors. For Wesley, it is clear that the neighbor is *anyone* and *everyone* else. Wesley advised:

> Seeing thou canst do all things through Christ strengthening thee, be merciful as thy Father in heaven is merciful. Love thy neighbour as thyself. Love friends and enemies as thy own soul. And let thy love be *long-suffering*, and patient towards all men. Let it be *kind*, soft, benign: inspiring thee with the most amiable sweetness, and the most fervent and tender affection. Let it 'rejoice in the truth', wheresoever it is found, the truth that is after godliness. Enjoy whatsoever brings glory to God, and promotes peace and goodwill among men. ("Sermon on the Mount, XIII," *Works*; Vol. 1, pages 697–98)

Wesley was fond of referring to what we do for others as "works of mercy" ("The Scripture Way of Salvation," *Works*; Vol. 2, page 166). These are rooted in God's love for us and our love for God. "Works of mercy" include anything related to the physical and spiritual condition of people:

> such as feeding the hungry, clothing the naked, entertaining the stranger, visiting those that are in prison, or sick, or variously afflicted; such as the endeavouring to instruct the ignorant, to awaken the ... sinner, to quicken the lukewarm, to confirm the wavering, to comfort the feebleminded, to succor the tempted, or contribute in any manner to the saving of souls from death. ("The Scripture Way of Salvation," *Works*; Vol. 2, page 166)

Convinced that faith without words and deeds that give evidence of faith is the "grand pest of Christianity" ("The Mystery of Iniquity," *Works*; Vol. 2, page 459), Wesley provided a set of "General Rules" that gave practical direction to Methodist people who were committed to holy living. These are still found in *The Book of Discipline of The United Methodist Church* and include three major points. First, Methodists are to do no harm to others and to avoid evil of every kind. Second, they are to do good to others, denying themselves, taking up the cross daily, and enduring the reproach that others may have for them because of their faith. Third, they are to utilize faithfully the "means of grace" that we have described above.

The goal of holiness is what Wesley called "Christian perfection," by which he meant having the mind of Christ. It means living life with one intention, namely that all our thoughts, words, and actions please God ("A Single Intention," *Works*; Vol. 4, pages 372–73). Love for God and neighbor becomes the controlling affection of our life. Nothing matters more! Christian perfection is nurtured by God's grace in "works of piety" and "works of mercy."

(7) The Way to Heaven

There was no doubt in Wesley's mind that God intends us to live eternally. As noted earlier, in the Preface to the published sermons, he wrote:

I am a creature of a day, passing through life as an arrow through air. I am a spirit come from God and returning to God; just hovering over the great gulf, till a few moments hence I am no more seen—I drop into an unchangeable eternity! I want to know one thing, the way to heaven—how to land safe on that happy shore. God himself has condescended to teach the way: for this very end he came from heaven. (Preface, *Works*; Vol. 1, pages 104–105)

Not only did Wesley want to know the way to heaven, he was also passionately committed to helping others find it as well. Holy living is the prelude to the fuller life available to all in Christ when the earthly journey is complete.

Wesley's sermons dwell much more on life in this world than on life in the next. However, that is not to underplay his belief that God has prepared a place for us beyond our life here on earth. Wesley's understanding of the Christian faith integrated salvation in this life and the next. He believed that the *only* way to heaven is through Jesus Christ. Jesus teaches us the way. Wesley wrote:

The Son of God, who came from heaven, [shows] us the way to heaven, to the place which he hath prepared for us, the glory he had before the world began. He [teaches] us the true way to life everlasting, the royal way which leads to the kingdom. And the only true way; for there is none besides—all other paths lead to destruction. ("Sermon on the Mount, I," *Works*; Vol. 1, page 470)

Jesus, of course, not only teaches the way to heaven, his sacrificial death opens the way. His Spirit leads and empowers us toward that end. The work of God for us and in us begun on earth continues and comes to completion in eternity.

Through the years Methodist hymns have celebrated the grace of the triune God and have anticipated the heavenly life for which the earthly life is an "antepast," a foretaste. Many of Charles Wesley's hymns speak of this reality in both this life and the next.

> O that I might so believe,
>   steadfastly to Jesus cleave,
> On his only love rely,
>   Smile at the destroyer nigh!
> Free from sin and service fear,
>   Have my Jesus ever near;
> All his care rejoice to prove,
>   All his paradise of love!
>
> Jesu, seek thy wandering sheep;
>   Bring me back, and lead, and keep;
> Take on my every care;
>   Bear me, on thy bosom bear.
> Let me know my Shepherd's voice,
>   More and more in thee rejoice;
> More and more of thee receive,
>   Ever in thy Spirit live.
>
> Live, till all thy life I know,
>   Perfect through my Lord below.
> Gladly then from earth remove,
>   Gathered to the fold above!
> O that I at last may stand
>   With the sheep at thy right hand,
> Take the crown so freely given,
>   Enter in by thee to heaven.
>   (*A Collection of Hymns*; 13)

Before leaving this section on holiness and sanctification, we must point out that in *The United Methodist Hymnal* there is a large section of hymns (382–536) that are designated hymns of "Sanctifying and Perfecting Grace."

ASSESSMENT

What can we say about the value of Wesley's Standard Sermons for our time? There are many reasons why there is value in paying attention to Wesley's Standard Sermons.

First, we need to remember what these sermons were intended to be. They are theological tracts that were designed by Wesley for theological nurture and reflection. They were not primarily meant to be read orally to a group or congregation, although there have been occasions over the years when they have been used in that way. Wesley understood that these published sermons required much more than simply to be heard. They needed to be studied, pondered, perhaps even argued with. We should recall their main purpose set forth in the introduction to the first edition of the sermons. The sermons were formulated to encourage and instruct new Christians in the basic ideas and realities of the Christian faith. Furthermore, they were published for people already committed to the faith who required the support and challenge that the sermons offered. Wesley, of course, contended that the sermons set forth the substance of his own preaching, teaching, and practice of the faith. They were expositions of what he considered essential to Christianity. Since the sermons are bathed in Scripture, Wesley also considered them worthy vehicles for presenting scriptural truth.

Second, the theological substance of the sermons is rich indeed, much richer than we have time and space to tell. We have spent relatively few pages dealing with the essence and meaning of the Standard Sermons. Nevertheless, we have suggested some of their main themes: original sin, prevenient grace, justification by faith, new birth, assurance, holiness of heart and life (including Christian perfection), and the way to heaven. We have found that, for Wesley, the holy life nurtured by God's grace must be the goal toward which every Christian aims. That holiness is nothing more than responding to God's grace by loving God with everything we are and have and loving our neighbors (everyone else) as we love ourselves.

Third, there is considerable value in reading and studying Wesley's Standard Sermons with care and seriousness. Someone recently mentioned to me that she had begun daily to read and study Wesley's sermons daily with great profit to her spiritual life. They deepened her faith and challenged her understanding and practice of it. She discovered that the sermons deal with everyday issues of entering into and living the Christian life.

There are 151 Standard Sermons. Not every sermon may be helpful to us, although all of them are worth our reading and consideration. For those who want to begin to read them, there are several sermons that are starting places. They include the following: "Salvation by Faith"; "The Scripture Way of Salvation"; "Scriptural Christianity"; "Free Grace"; "Justification by Faith"; "The New Birth"; "The Marks of the New Birth"; "Christian Perfection"; "Catholic Spirit"; "The Means of Grace"; "The Duty of Constant Communion"; "The Danger of Riches"; "The Use of Money"; and four sermons "Upon our Lord's Sermon on the Mount, IV, V, VI, VII." These sermons may be found in almost every recent edition of Wesley's works, including the Bicentennial Edition (which is the only edition to have all 151 sermons) and various collections, including *John Wesley's Sermons: An Anthology*, edited by Albert C. Outler and Richard P. Heitzenrater (paperback, Abingdon Press, 1991), which includes fifty of the sermons carefully chosen to illuminate the main thrust of Wesley's thought.

One who wants to read the sermons must be prepared to persevere through the eighteenth-century English in which they were written. However, patience with the language of the sermons will be rewarded as one reads more of them and discerns a plain pattern in many of them. The reader will also have to be ready for occasional Greek or Latin language quotes. These do not in any way detract from the text of the sermons, and the reader should not be put off by them.

Furthermore, although Wesley argued that he labored to avoid what he called speculation and "perplexed and intricate reasonings," there are a few places in the sermons where he seems to have succumbed to that temptation. One such is his early (1726) sermon "On Guardian Angels," in which he attempted to describe in rather speculative fashion these messengers of God and their work on behalf of humans ("On Guardian Angels," *Works*; Vol. 4, pages 224–35). Yet even the speculative sections of his sermons are provocative, challenging, and instructive.

CONCLUSION

Wesley's Standard Sermons are one of the most important sources of United Methodism's doctrinal heritage. They present us with what Wesley considered the most significant ideas of the Christian faith. He intended that they provide a guide for Methodists regarding what they should believe and what they should do in order to please God and to fulfill God's purpose in their lives. The sermons show Wesley's devotion to Scripture, tradition, reason, and experience as sources for understanding Christianity and its unique embodiment in Methodism. They contain a wealth of inspirational and practical direction for United Methodist disciples in the twenty-first century, especially when read and studied with the other three doctrinal standards.

Some Questions for Reflection and Discussion

(1) Before reading this chapter, what did you know about the published sermons of John Wesley? Have you ever seen or read any of them? What do you think about his use of published sermons as a way to teach people the major themes of the Christian faith?

(2) Grace is a main emphasis of Wesleyan theology. How do you define grace? John Wesley spoke about it as prevenient grace, justifying grace, and sanctifying grace. How would you say that each of these dimensions of grace has been, and is, present in your life?

(3) We hear a lot about being a "born again" Christian. What does that mean? Can Wesley's views on the new birth help us understand this important Christian theme?

(4) One of the "means of grace," or "works of piety," for Wesley was fasting. Have you ever engaged in fasting as a spiritual discipline? Why did you fast? Can our sense of God's presence be strengthened by fasting?

(5) Wesley believed that it is difficult to be Christians "all by ourselves." In what ways do you share your pilgrimage of faith with other Christians? What advantages have you discovered in sharing in Christian fellowship with others? What do you believe you have contributed to their pilgrimage, and what have they contributed to yours?

(6) The Lord's Supper was important to Wesley as a means by which God's sustaining grace was conveyed into his life. What does the Lord's Supper mean to you? How often do you receive it? Should our churches offer more occasions for celebrating the Lord's Supper?

(7) John Wesley believed that we should all engage in "works of mercy." These not only minister to the needs of others, they are also a means by which God nurtures our faith. They may be viewed as an obligation and a gift. In what ways do you engage in "works of mercy"? How does your church engage in them?

(8) We hear many more sermons than we read. Of what importance is preaching to you? When was the last time God spoke to you through preaching?

SUGGESTIONS FOR FURTHER READING AND STUDY

Collins, Kenneth J. *The Scripture Way of Salvation: The Heart of John Wesley's Theology*. Nashville: Abingdon Press, 1997. Introduces the main themes of Wesley's theology with an emphasis on his sermons.

Outler, Albert C. *John Wesley's Sermons: An Introduction*. Nashville: Abingdon Press, 1991. Reprint of the introductory essay in the sermons volumes of the Bicentennial Edition of Wesley's Works. Discusses Wesley as preacher, his theological method, and the sources from which he drew his interpretation of the Christian faith and life.

Outler, Albert C. and Richard P. Heitzenrater. *John Wesley's Sermons: An Anthology*. Nashville: Abingdon Press, 1991. Contains the full text of fifty of Wesley's sermons that Outler and Heitzenrater have chosen as most important.

Wesley, John. *The Works of John Wesley*. Bicentennial Edition. Vols. I, II, III, IV edited with introduction by Albert C. Outler. Nashville: Abingdon Press, 1984–1987. These volumes include all the known published sermons of John Wesley. The footnoting identifies the location of scriptural quotes and provides other important documentation. The four sermons volumes are also available on CD with excellent word and phrase search capabilities.

Wesley, John. *The Works of John Wesley*. Grand Rapids, MI: Baker Book House, 1979. Reprint of the 1831 Thomas Jackson edition of Wesley's Works including most, but not all, of the sermons. This edition has also been placed on a CD with excellent word and phrase search capabilities.

---

[1] All quotations from *Works*, unless otherwise indicated are from *The Works of John Wesley*, Vols. 1–4, edited by Albert C. Outler (Abingdon Press, 1984–1987).

[2] From *A History of The Methodist Church in Great Britain*, Vol. 4 (Epworth Press); page 151.

[3] From *The Doctrine of Original Sin*, in *The Works of John Wesley*, Vol. IX (Baker Book House, 1979); page 335.

[4] From *The Principles of a Methodist Farther Explained*, in *The Works of John Wesley*, Vol. 9, edited by Rupert E. Davier (Abingdon Press, 1989); page 227.

[5] From "Hymn on the Means of Grace," in *The Poetical Works of John and Charles Wesley*, Vol. III (Wesleyan-Methodist Conference Office, 1870); page 440.

CHAPTER 3
THE ARTICLES OF RELIGION OF THE METHODIST CHURCH

The Articles of Religion of The Methodist Church are the third doctrinal standard of The United Methodist Church. Since there are only twenty-five Articles, accompanied by two unnumbered items, their complete text is found in *The Book of Discipline of The United Methodist Church*. They have been prominently placed in the Methodist *Discipline* since 1788. For more than two centuries the Articles have functioned as important doctrinal statements of the denomination.

HISTORICAL BACKGROUND

Like the *Explanatory Notes Upon the New Testament* and the Standard Sermons, United Methodism's Articles of Religion owe their origin to John Wesley. In 1784, Wesley allowed Methodists in the newly formed United States to organize their own church, which they called The Methodist Episcopal Church. He dispatched three of his preachers to America with a published worship book that he entitled *The Sunday Service of the Methodists in North America. With Other Occasional Services*. He included in this book a document entitled "Articles of Religion." These Articles were Wesley's edited version of the Thirty-nine Articles of the Church of England. To this day the Thirty-nine Articles are considered an important doctrinal statement of basic Anglican theology.

The Church of England's Thirty-nine Articles have a rich history. Their roots may be traced to Lutheranism's Augsburg Confession, drafted in 1530. Earlier versions of the Thirty-nine Articles were the Ten Articles (1536), the Thirteen Articles (1538), and the Forty-two Articles (1553). In 1571, the Church of England adopted the Thirty-nine Articles. They were believed to teach the truths of the Bible and the major creeds of the church, including the Apostles' Creed and the Nicene Creed, two early summaries of Christian belief.

Since John Wesley considered himself a loyal clergyman of the Church of England, it is not surprising that he considered the Thirty-nine Articles important doctrinal statements. We must, however, also note that when he edited them down to the twenty-four that he sent to the American Methodists, he omitted some of the Thirty-nine Articles entirely and made changes in others. For example, missing from Wesley's version are the Articles on Christ's descent into hell, predestination and election, avoiding excommunicated church members, and the consecration of bishops and ministers. These omissions probably reflected his view that the content of some of the Articles was confusing or questionable and that others were not pertinent to the American situation. Even in the Articles he retained, Wesley omitted sections in some and made word or phrase changes in others. For example, in the Article that speaks about and lists the names of the books of the Old Testament, Wesley omitted the reference to and list of the Apocrypha. Many of his changes were simply made to make the Article read more easily. For example, in Article II, he altered the phrase "The Son, *which* is the Word of the Father" to "The Son, *who* is the Word of the Father."

After Wesley's twenty-four Articles of Religion were received in 1784 by the American Methodists, another Article was added (now Article XXIII); it deals with the government of the United States. A few other minor changes to the Articles were subsequently made by the American Methodist Episcopal Church in the early nineteenth century.

When The Methodist Episcopal Church drafted its first Constitution in 1808, they included an important "Restrictive Rule" that protected the Articles of Religion and other "standards of doctrine." This provision remains in the Constitution of The United Methodist Church and reads as follows:

> The General Conference shall not revoke, alter, or change our Articles of Religion or establish any new standards or rules of doctrine contrary to our present existing and established standards of doctrine. (*Book of Discipline*; Para. 16)

It is worth observing at this point that there are some scholars, led by Professor Richard P. Heitzenrater, who believe that there is compelling evidence that in the early nineteenth century, American Methodists considered the Articles of Religion to be their only binding doctrinal standard. Other scholars, following Thomas Oden, have argued that the *Explanatory Notes Upon the New Testament* and Wesley's Standard Sermons, as well as the Articles of Religion, have always been considered the standards of doctrine in Methodism, including American Methodism. To read more about this debate, see the works by Richard P. Heitzenrater and Thomas Oden in the suggested reading list at the end of this chapter. While the Heitzenrater/Oden discussion is both interesting and informative, we must remember that United Methodism today considers all three of these—the *Notes*, sermons, and Articles—among its four doctrinal standards. All three are given that status in *The Book of Discipline*.

CONTENT

Since the Articles of Religion are relatively short, their complete text as printed in *The Book of Discipline of The United Methodist Church* is found below in bold type. The Articles may be grouped into five major categories: The Triune God (Articles I–IV); Scripture (Articles V–VI); Sin and Salvation (Articles VII–XII); Church and Sacraments (Articles XIII–XXII); and the Christian in Society (Articles XXIII–XXV). Comments will be offered for each set of Articles as well as for the two unnumbered paragraphs published at the end of the Articles in *The Book of Discipline*.

(1) The Triune God (Articles I–IV)

Article I—Of Faith in the Holy Trinity
There is but one living and true God, everlasting, without body or parts, of infinite power, wisdom, and goodness; the maker and preserver of all things, both visible and invisible. And in unity of this Godhead there are three persons, of one substance, power, and eternity— the Father, the Son, and the Holy Ghost.

Article II—Of the Word, or Son of God, Who Was Made Very Man
The Son, who is the Word of the Father, the very and eternal God, of one substance with the Father, took man's nature in the womb of the blessed Virgin; so that two whole and perfect natures, that is to say, the Godhead and Manhood, were joined together in one person, never to be divided; whereof is one Christ, very God and very Man, who truly suffered, was crucified, dead, and buried, to reconcile his Father to us, and to be a sacrifice, not only for original guilt, but also for actual sins of men.

Article III—Of the Resurrection of Christ
Christ did truly rise again from the dead, and took again his body, with all things appertaining to the perfection of man's nature, wherewith he ascended into heaven, and there sitteth until he return to judge all men at the last day.

Article IV—Of the Holy Ghost

The Holy Ghost, proceeding from the Father and the Son, is of one substance, majesty, and glory with the Father and the Son, very and eternal God.

This cluster of Articles offers a forceful affirmation about the being and nature of God. **Article I** opens with the statement that there is only "one living and true God." It reiterates the basic monotheism (belief in one God) that is at the center of the Judeo-Christian faith, the God who is spoken about in both Testaments of the Bible. God is "everlasting," having no beginning and no end. God is "without body or parts," having no material shape and not confined to space or time as humans are. God's "power, wisdom, and goodness" are limitless. The next phrase speaks about God as "the maker and preserver of all things, both visible and invisible." This is reminiscent of the ancient Apostles' and Nicene creeds used regularly in the worship of many congregations. In the Apostles' Creed we say,

> I believe in God the Father Almighty,
> maker of heaven and earth.

In the Nicene Creed we state,

> We believe in one God,
> the Father, the Almighty,
> maker of heaven and earth,
> and of all that is, seen and unseen.

At the close of **Article I**, there is an important assertion of the trinitarian nature of God in whom "there are three persons, of one substance, power, and eternity—the Father, the Son, and the Holy Ghost." We have already pointed out that in the *Notes* and sermons, John Wesley was clear in embracing the traditional trinitarian understanding of God. Wesley used traditional trinitarian language by referring to God as Father, Son, and Holy Ghost. One of the controversies in the church today has to do with this traditional language formula—Father, Son, and Holy Ghost—that many people find problematic. They prefer terminology such as "Creator, Redeemer, Sustainer" because this language is more inclusive. Others feel that the traditional language formula is both biblically correct and consistent with Christian tradition. For example, they cite the baptismal formula in Matthew 28:19-20, which quotes Jesus as saying that his disciples should be baptized "in the name of the Father and of the Son and of the Holy Spirit."

Articles II and **III** speak specifically about Jesus Christ, the second person of the Trinity. In **Article II**, Jesus is described as "the Word of the Father," a direct reference to the opening chapter of the Gospel of John, where Jesus is called "the Word" (John 1:1-14). The Article announces that Jesus is "the very and eternal God, of one substance with the Father." This statement underscores Jesus' divinity, that is, that Jesus is the second person of the triune God. Next, Jesus' humanity is declared by stating that he "took man's nature in the womb of the blessed Virgin." In Jesus, therefore, the divine and the human were perfectly united. The Article puts it this way: "Two whole and perfect natures, that is to say, the Godhead and Manhood, were joined together in one person, never to be divided; whereof is one Christ, very God and very Man." Although this is a plain statement, it does not reveal the complexity of the mystery (the union of full divinity and full humanity in Jesus) and the many decades of debate in the early church over the relation of Christ's divinity and humanity. Another way of describing the union of the divine and human in Jesus is the theological term *Incarnation*, which has to do with the "enfleshment" of God in a human body. Charles Wesley wrote many hymns to celebrate that union.

> Let earth and heaven combine,
>   Angels and men agree,
> To praise in songs divine the incarnate Deity,
>   Our God contracted to a span,
> Incomprehensibly made man.
>
> He laid his glory by,
>   He wrapped him in our clay,
> Unmarked by human eye,
>   The latent Godhead lay,
> Infant of days he here became;
> And bore the mild Immanuel's name.
>
> See in that infant's face the depths of Deity,
> And labour while ye gaze,
>   To sound the mystery;
> In vain: ye angels gaze no more,
> But fall and silently adore.

Unsearchable the love,
   That hath the Saviour brought,
The grace is far above,
   Or man or angel's thought:
Suffice for us that God we know,
Our God is manifest below.

He deigns in Flesh to appear,
   Widest Extremes to join,
To bring our Vileness near,
   And make us All divine;
And we the Life of GOD shall know,
For God is manifest below.

Made perfect first in love,
   And sanctified by Grace,
We shall from Earth remove,
   And see his glorious face;
His love shall then be fully showed,
And man shall all be lost in God.[1]

Article II closes with a statement about the reason for the coupling of the human and divine in Jesus. He "truly suffered, was crucified, dead, and buried, to reconcile his Father to us, and to be a sacrifice, not only for original guilt, but also for [the] actual sins of men." There are two key actions in which Jesus engages. First, in Jesus, God becomes like us so that we might become like God. Second, Jesus' death is a sacrificial offering for our guilt and sin, opening the way for a full restoration of relationship with God.

Article III announces the resurrection of Christ. He "did truly rise again from the dead, and took again his body, with all things appertaining to the perfection of man's nature." The resurrection of Christ was proclaimed by the earliest Christians as God's triumph over the world's evil powers and human sinfulness. The message of Jesus' resurrection is not only announced throughout the New Testament but is also declared in the church's creeds and hymns. On "the third day he rose from the dead," we state in the Apostles' Creed. The Nicene Creed says it in a little different way:

On the third day he rose again
in accordance with the Scriptures.

Who of us is not stirred when we sing Charles Wesley's words about Christ's resurrection *and ours*.

> Christ the Lord is risen today,
> Alleluia!
> Earth and heaven in chorus say,
> Alleluia!
> Raise your joys and triumphs high,
> Alleluia!
> Sing, ye heavens, and earth reply,
> Alleluia!
>
> Love's redeeming work is done,
> Alleluia!
> Fought the fight, the battle won,
> Alleluia!
> Death in vain forbids him rise,
> Alleluia!
> Christ has opened paradise,
> Alleluia!
>
> Lives again our glorious King,
> Alleluia!
> Where, O death, is now thy sting?
> Alleluia!
> Once he died our souls to save,
> Alleluia!
> Where's thy victory, boasting grave?
> Alleluia!
>
> Soar we now where Christ has led,
> Alleluia!
> Following our exalted Head,
> Alleluia!
> Made like him, like him we rise,
> Alleluia!
> Ours the cross, the grave, the skies,
> Alleluia!
> (*The United Methodist Hymnal;* 302)

Jesus was not only raised from the dead; as **Article III** states, "he ascended into heaven" and will "return to judge all men at the last day."

Articles II and **III** tell about the triune God's reconciling acts in Jesus Christ, the second person of the Trinity.

Finally, **Article IV** speaks about the Holy Ghost (Holy Spirit), the third person of the Trinity. Although the Spirit of God is spoken of frequently in the Old Testament (for example, Judges 3:10; 2 Samuel 23:2; Isaiah 11:2; Joel 2:28-29), it was in the earliest Christian community that the Holy Spirit of God, a fresh and powerful outpouring of God's presence, became an undeniable and essential reality in the life of the Christian believer and the church. This gift of the Holy Spirit to God's people, promised in Joel 2:28-29, filled, inspired, empowered, and directed the early Christians (Acts 2). The presence and work of the Holy Spirit is attested throughout the rest of the New Testament. Our creeds speak of the Holy Spirit.

> We believe in the Holy Spirit, the Lord, the giver of life,
> who proceeds from the Father and the Son,
> who with the Father and the Son
> is worshiped and glorified,
> who has spoken through the prophets.
> (Nicene Creed)

The Korean Creed (*The United Methodist Hymnal*; 884) has another way of expressing the Spirit's role:

> We believe in the Holy Spirit,
> God present with us for guidance, for comfort, and for strength.

Charles Wesley spoke about the important place and action of the Holy Spirit in one of his most familiar prayer-hymns:

> Come, Holy Ghost, our hearts inspire,
> let us thine influence prove;
> source of the old prophetic fire,
> fountain of life and love.
> . . . .
> Expand thy wings, celestial Dove,
> brood o'er our nature's night;
> on our disordered spirits move,
> and let there now be light.

God, through the Spirit we shall know
if thou within us shine,
and sound, with all thy saints below,
the depths of love divine.
(*The United Methodist Hymnal*; 603)

(2) Scripture (Articles V–VI)

Article V—Of the Sufficiency of the Holy Scriptures for Salvation

The Holy Scripture containeth all things necessary to salvation; so that whatsoever is not read therein, nor may be proved thereby, is not to be required of any man that it should be believed as an article of faith, or be thought requisite or necessary to salvation. In the name of the Holy Scripture we do understand those canonical books of the Old and New Testament of whose authority was never any doubt in the church. The names of the canonical books are:

Genesis, Exodus, Leviticus, Numbers, Deuteronomy, Joshua, Judges, Ruth, The First Book of Samuel, The Second Book of Samuel, The First Book of Kings, The Second Book of Kings, The First Book of Chronicles, The Second Book of Chronicles, The Book of Ezra, The Book of Nehemiah, The Book of Esther, The Book of Job, The Psalms, The Proverbs, Ecclesiastes or the Preacher, Cantica or Songs of Solomon, Four Prophets the Greater, Twelve Prophets the Less.

All the books of the New Testament, as they are commonly received, we do receive and account canonical.

Article VI—Of the Old Testament

The Old Testament is not contrary to the New; for both in the Old and New Testament everlasting life is offered to mankind by Christ, who is the only Mediator between God and man, being both God and Man. Wherefore they are not to be heard who feign that the old fathers did look only for transitory promises. Although the law given from God by Moses as touching ceremonies and rights doth not bind Christians, nor ought the civil precepts thereof of necessity be received in any commonwealth; yet notwithstanding, no Christian whatsoever is free from the obedience of the commandments which are called moral.

Articles V and VI state the importance of the Bible, the Holy Scriptures, for Christians and the Christian community, the church. The message of the Bible is the message of salvation. The Scriptures tell the story of Creation, human failing, God's gracious forgiveness and reconciliation, and new life for individuals and the human community. The Scriptures are the basis of what we believe and do as people of God.

We observed earlier that John Wesley referred to himself as *homo unius libri*, a man of one book, the Bible. No other book was more important to him. United Methodism continues in this tradition by giving the Bible the highest place among the sources from which we draw our understanding and practice of the faith. The United Methodist Church officially says about the Bible:

> United Methodists share with other Christians the conviction that Scripture is the primary source and criterion for Christian doctrine. Through Scripture the living Christ meets us in the experience of redeeming grace. We are convinced that Jesus Christ is the living Word of God in our midst whom we trust in life and death.
>
> The biblical authors, illumined by the Holy Spirit, bear witness that in Christ the world is reconciled to God. The Bible bears authentic testimony to God's self-disclosure in the life, death, and resurrection of Jesus Christ as well as in God's work of creation, in the pilgrimage of Israel, and in the Holy Spirit's ongoing activity in human history.
>
> As we open our minds and hearts to the Word of God through the words of human beings inspired by the Holy Spirit, faith is born and nourished, our understanding is deepened, and the possibilities for transforming the world become apparent to us. ("Our Theological Task," *Book of Discipline*; Para. 63)

Article V lists the canonical books of the Old Testament. The term *canonical* here means those inspired books that the church considers Holy Scripture. The four "Greater" prophets include Isaiah, Jeremiah, Ezekiel, and Daniel. The "Lesser" prophets include Hosea, Joel, Amos, Obadiah, Jonah, Micah, Nahum, Habakkuk, Zephaniah, Haggai, Zechariah, Malachi. The Old Testament Book of Lamentations, thought to have been written by Jeremiah, is included among the "Greater" prophets. This list, therefore, includes the thirty-nine books that are presently incorporated into the Old Testament. **Article V** does not list the New Testament books by name. It simply acknowledges the twenty-seven books that have been considered canonical since the fourth century.

Article VI speaks more specifically about the Old Testament. It affirms that the two Testaments are not in opposition to each other. Both Testaments also bear testimony to Jesus Christ as the *only* Mediator between

God and the human race. Holy people in Old Testament times looked forward to the promised Messiah, the Christ, an anticipation realized in Jesus of Nazareth. The Article closes with the statement that Christians are not bound by the ceremonial and ritual laws of the Old Testament, nor by provisions related to any civil law that pertained solely to pre-Christian times. However, it is quite clearly stated that "no Christian whatsoever is free from the obedience of the commandments which are called moral." These include, for example, the Ten Commandments, which are a central part of the moral law. The moral law is to be kept by the disciples of Christ.

(3) Sin and Salvation (Articles VII–XII)

Article VII—Of Original or Birth Sin

Original sin standeth not in the following of Adam (as the Pelagians do vainly talk), but it is the corruption of the nature of every man, that naturally is engendered of the offspring of Adam, whereby man is very far gone from original righteousness, and of his own nature inclined to evil, and that continually.

Article VIII—Of Free Will

The condition of man after the fall of Adam is such that he cannot turn and prepare himself, by his own natural strength and works, to faith, and calling upon God; wherefore we have no power to do good works, pleasant and acceptable to God, without the grace of God by Christ preventing us, that we may have a good will, and working with us, when we have that good will.

Article IX—Of the Justification of Man

We are accounted righteous before God only for the merit of our Lord and Saviour Jesus Christ, by faith, and not for our own works or deservings. Wherefore, that we are justified by faith, only, is a most wholesome doctrine, and very full of comfort.

Article X—Of Good Works

Although good works, which are the fruits of faith, and follow after justification, cannot put away our sins, and endure the severity of God's judgment; yet are they pleasing and acceptable to God in Christ, and spring out of a true and lively faith, insomuch that by them a lively faith may be as evidently known as a tree is discerned by its fruit.

Article XI—Of Works of Supererogation

Voluntary works—besides, over and above God's commandments—which they call works of supererogation, cannot be taught without arrogancy and impiety. For by them men do declare that they do not only render unto God as much as they are bound to do, but that they do more for his sake than of bounden duty is required; whereas Christ saith plainly: When you have done all that is commanded you, say, We are unprofitable servants.

Article XII—Of Sin After Justification

Not every sin willingly committed after justification is the sin against the Holy Ghost, and unpardonable. Wherefore, the grant of repentance is not to be denied to such as fall into sin after justification. After we have received the Holy Ghost, we may depart from grace given, and fall into sin, and, by the grace of God, rise again and amend our lives. And therefore they are to be condemned who say they can no more sin as long as they live here; or deny the place of forgiveness to such as truly repent.

We have already pointed out that sin is considered with utmost seriousness in Wesley's *Notes* and sermons. It is also mentioned prominently in the Articles. **Article VII** begins by mentioning the Pelagians. They were the followers of Pelagius, a fifth-century British monk who held that human beings are free not to sin even though they have a tendency to follow the disobedience of Adam. The Article asserts that the human situation is much more ominous. From the earliest days of human history, *all of us* have suffered from a disease. This illness involves "the corruption of the nature of every man, that naturally is engendered of the offspring of Adam, whereby man is very far gone from original righteousness, and of his own nature inclined to evil, and that continually." We stand in rebellion against God. We do what God says we must not do. We fail to do what God says we should do. The righteousness and holiness that God demands of us, that would result in proper relationships with God and our neighbors, we are incapable of fulfilling. We are "very far gone" from the righteous life God intends for each and all of us. Our sickness involves our inclination to do evil rather than good.

It is a great temptation for each of us to take too lightly the ways in which we fail to be the people God wants us to be. We hesitate to consider ourselves "unrighteous" and "sinful." We prefer to think, *We aren't too bad.* This Article presents a different view. It describes us as deeply mired in a condition from which we are unable to extricate ourselves. The apostle Paul described our dilemma in Romans 7:24: "Wretched man that I am! Who will rescue me from this body of death?"

Article VIII underscores the desperation of our condition by stating that because of sin, we are not free to "turn and prepare" ourselves to accept God's cure for our disease. Furthermore, we are unable to do that which is pleasing to God and to do good to our neighbors. None of this is possible *except* by "the grace of God by Christ preventing us." Here we have a clear word about God's "preventing" (prevenient) grace, an emphasis that we observed earlier, especially in Wesley's sermons. God's prevenient, or preparing, grace stirs us to understand our sinful condition, illuminates the way to new life, *frees* us to accept God's forgiveness and reconciliation, moves us to repentance and genuine change, and leads us to do good works. God's prevenient grace, literally "the grace that comes before," is the beginning of good news for all people. It is the grace that surrounds and inhabits all people even when it is not recognized. Prevenient grace is the first step in our healing.

Some other theological traditions have denied that humans are free to respond to the saving grace God offers in Christ. Martin Luther (1483–1547), the leader of the Protestant Reformation, spoke about the "bondage of the will." Sin has so corrupted the human will, he believed, that it is not free to respond to the saving grace of God in Christ. The Wesleyan tradition affirms the substance of **Article VIII**. God's grace is free for all and opens the path to freedom and to further and necessary expressions of divine grace.

The problem addressed in **Article IX** is how unrighteous people stand before a righteous God. How can the unjust, that is, those who do what is wrong and fail to do what is right, be acceptable to God? How can we be justified? The Article reminds us that we neither earn nor deserve God's acceptance. Our being treated as righteous and just people completely depends upon our acceptance and faithful trust in what God does for us in Jesus Christ, our Lord and Savior. God does for us what we cannot do for ourselves. The biblical message reminds us that we are justified, forgiven, and accepted by God on the basis of our trust in God's grace, which is freely available to all. This is an especially clear theme in the writings of Paul. In his letter to the Romans, for example, he wrote that "we are justified by faith" (5:1).

Justification by faith is a prominent theme in John Wesley's *Notes* and sermons. His views on this matter are well stated in his sermon "The Scripture Way of Salvation," in which he wrote that justification

is the forgiveness of all our sins, and . . . our acceptance with God. The price whereby this hath been procured for us (commonly termed the 'meritorious cause' of our justification) is the blood and righteousness of Christ, or (to express it a little more clearly) all that Christ hath done and suffered for us till 'he poured out his soul for the transgressors.' ("The Scripture Way of Salvation," *Works*; Vol. 2, pages 155–56)

These words of Wesley amplify the substance of **Article IX**.

Article X reminds us that although good works are not sufficient to earn our right standing with God, they should "spring out of a true and lively faith." Just as a vigorous and healthy tree is known by the fruit it bears, so genuine faith in a Christian and in the Christian community is made evident in words and acts.

One of the hallmarks of Wesleyan/Methodist theology is the close relationship of faith and works. Many centuries ago, the writer of the Letter of James wrote this to his readers:

> What good is it, my brothers and sisters, if you say you have faith but do not have works? Can faith save you? If a brother or sister is naked and lacks daily food, and one of you says to them, "Go in peace; keep warm and eat your fill," and yet you do not supply their bodily needs, what is the good of that? So faith by itself, if it has no works, is dead.
>
> But someone will say, "You have faith and I have works." Show me your faith apart from your works, and I by my works will show you my faith. (James 2:14-18)

Wesley often referred to the good works we do for others as "works of mercy." He urged his followers to do "works of mercy" whenever and wherever they could. They are testimonies to a holy life and, as **Article X** asserts, they are "pleasing and acceptable to God in Christ." The opportunities to engage in faithful works are limitless. They include everything from visiting and comforting the sick and prisoners to offering food and clothing to the poor at soup kitchens and clothing centers. We could never provide here a complete list of the "works of mercy" that you and your church can supply as a testimony to your faith. New opportunities to do them arise daily.

Article XI uses the term *supererogation*, a strange word to our vocabulary. Supererogation refers to doing more good works than God expects of us. The idea that we can do good "besides, over and above God's commandments" is both arrogant and impious. Rather, we must recall the counsel of Christ that when we have done everything commanded of us, we still say,

"We are unprofitable servants." We can never do more than enough in faithful response to God's grace. Yet, when we have done all we can do, God's grace is more than sufficient for our needs and our salvation.

The final item in this cluster, **Article XII**, addresses the problem of our disobedience and sin after we have been prepared by grace and have accepted God's offer of pardon and forgiveness (justifying grace) by faith. The Article refers to the "unpardonable" sin, the sin against the Holy Spirit that is mentioned in the Gospel of Mark: "Whoever blasphemes against the Holy Spirit can never have forgiveness, but is guilty of an eternal sin" (3:29). Those who deliberately and stubbornly turn away from God's truth and who refuse to respond to God's offer of saving grace cannot be pardoned. However, after justification, any of us "may depart from grace given, and fall into sin, and, by the grace of God, rise again and amend our lives." In this Article there is a plain denial of what some call "eternal security" or "once saved, always saved," which claims that once people have received the saving grace of God, they cannot lose their salvation.

The last two phrases of the Article are important. The first indicates that those who say they can no longer sin after they have been justified (called in Wesley's day "antinomianism"—the belief that one has no need of the moral law) are perpetuating a fantasy and are to be condemned. The second advises not to "deny the place of forgiveness to [any who] truly repent."

(4) Church and Sacraments (Articles XIII–XXII)

Article XIII—Of the Church
The visible church of Christ is a congregation of faithful men in which the pure Word of God is preached, and the Sacraments duly administered according to Christ's ordinance, in all those things that of necessity are requisite to the same.

Article XIV—Of Purgatory
The Romish doctrine concerning purgatory, pardon, worshiping, and adoration, as well of images as of relics, and also invocation of saints, is a fond thing, vainly invented, and grounded upon no warrant of Scripture, but repugnant to the Word of God.

Article XV—Of Speaking in the Congregation in Such a Tongue as the People Understand
It is a thing plainly repugnant to the Word of God, and the custom of the primitive church, to have public prayer in the church, or to minister the Sacraments, in a tongue not understood by the people.

Article XVI—Of the Sacraments

Sacraments ordained of Christ are not only badges or tokens of Christian men's profession, but rather they are certain signs of grace, and God's good will toward us, by which he doth work invisibly in us, and doth not only quicken, but also strengthen and confirm, our faith in him.

There are two Sacraments ordained of Christ our Lord in the Gospel; that is to say, Baptism and the Supper of the Lord.

Those five commonly called sacraments, that is to say, confirmation, penance, orders, matrimony, and extreme unction, are not to be counted for Sacraments of the Gospel; being such as have partly grown out of the *corrupt* following of the apostles, and partly are states of life allowed in the Scriptures, but yet have not the like nature of Baptism and the Lord's Supper, because they have not any visible sign or ceremony ordained of God.

The Sacraments were not ordained of Christ to be gazed upon, or to be carried about; but that we should duly use them. And in such only as worthily receive the same, they have a wholesome effect or operation; but they that receive them unworthily, purchase to themselves condemnation, as St. Paul saith.

Article XVII—Of Baptism

Baptism is not only a sign of profession and mark of difference whereby Christians are distinguished from others that are not baptized; but it is also a sign of regeneration or the new birth. The Baptism of young children is to be retained in the Church.

Article XVIII—Of the Lord's Supper

The Supper of the Lord is not only a sign of the love that Christians ought to have among themselves one to another, but rather is a sacrament of our redemption by Christ's death; insomuch that, to such as rightly, worthily, and with faith receive the same, the bread which we break is a partaking of the body of Christ; and likewise the cup of blessing is a partaking of the blood of Christ.

Transubstantiation, or the change of the substance of bread and wine in the Supper of our Lord, cannot be proved by Holy Writ, but is repugnant to the plain words of Scripture, overthroweth the nature of a sacrament, and hath given occasion to many superstitions.

The body of Christ is given, taken, and eaten in the Supper, only after a heavenly and spiritual manner. And the mean whereby the body of Christ is received and eaten in the Supper is faith.

The Sacrament of the Lord's Supper was not by Christ's ordinance reserved, carried about, lifted up, or worshiped.

Article XIX—Of Both Kinds

The cup of the Lord is not to be denied to the lay people; for both the parts of the Lord's Supper, by Christ's ordinance and commandment, ought to be administered to all Christians alike.

Article XX—Of the One Oblation of Christ, Finished Upon the Cross

The offering of Christ, once made, is that perfect redemption, propitiation, and satisfaction for all the sins of the whole world, both original and actual; and there is none other satisfaction for sin but that alone. Wherefore the sacrifice of masses, in the which it is commonly said that the priest doth offer Christ for the quick and the dead, to have remission of pain or guilt, is a blasphemous fable and dangerous deceit.

Article XXI—Of the Marriage of Ministers

The ministers of Christ are not commanded by God's law either to vow the estate of single life, or to abstain from marriage; therefore it is lawful for them, as for all other Christians, to marry at their own discretion, as they shall judge the same to serve best to godliness.

Article XXII—Of the Rites and Ceremonies of Churches

It is not necessary that rites and ceremonies should in all places be the same, or exactly alike; for they have been always different, and may be changed according to the diversity of countries, times, and men's manners, so that nothing be ordained against God's Word. Whosoever, through his private judgment, willingly and purposely doth openly break the rites and ceremonies of the church to which he belongs, which are not repugnant to the Word of God, and are ordained and approved by common authority, ought to be rebuked openly, that others may fear to do the like, as one that offendeth against the common order of the church, and woundeth the consciences of weak brethren.

Every particular church may ordain, change, or abolish rites and ceremonies, so that all things may be done to edification.

This cluster of Articles dealing with the church and the sacraments includes several that reflect anti-Roman Catholic views. This is especially true of all or part of **Articles XIV, XV, XVI, XVIII, XIX, XX,** and **XXI.** The references to Roman Catholicism demonstrate an understanding of that church that was held by the Church of England when the original Thirty-nine Articles were drafted in 1571. They also reflect Wesley's own convictions about the Roman Catholic Church in 1784 when he revised the

Anglican Articles for America. The 1970 General Conference of The United Methodist Church recognized the necessity to speak about the polemical bias against Roman Catholicism in these Articles and passed the following resolution:

> Therefore, be it hereby resolved that we declare it our official intent henceforth to interpret *all* our Articles, Confession, and other "standards of doctrine" in consonance with our best ecumenical insights and judgment. . . . This implies, as the very least, our heartiest offer of goodwill and Christian brotherhood to all our Roman Catholic brethren, in the avowed hope of the day when all bitter memories (ours and theirs) will have been redeemed by the gift of the fullness of Christian unity, from the God and Father of our common Lord, Jesus Christ.[2]

When we considered Wesley's *Notes* in an earlier chapter, we pointed out that some of his comments, especially on the Book of Revelation, contain heated references against the Roman Catholic Church and the papacy. However, in other places, Wesley was conciliatory toward Roman Catholics. In his "Letter to a Roman Catholic," published in 1749, he urged Protestants and Catholics to do nothing to "hurt one another," "to speak nothing harsh or unkind of each other," to "harbour no unkind thought, no unfriendly temper, towards each other," and to "endeavor to help each other on in whatever . . . leads to the kingdom." United Methodists today, recognizing that Roman Catholic believers are their sisters and brothers in the faith, will want to join with them in the witness of doing God's will in the world while recognizing that there remain among them some significant differences in doctrine and practice.

Article XIII offers a traditional definition of the church as the community of faithful people in which the Word of God is preached and the sacraments properly administered. The necessary existence of a faithful community of God's people is a central fact of the Judeo-Christian tradition. In Judaism this community encompassed all who worshiped and served Yahweh, the Holy One of Israel, who created and sustained the community. The early Christian church understood itself to include all who believed God's revelation in Jesus Christ and who followed him as Savior and Lord. It was difficult for them to think of themselves as "private" Christians. They were drawn together by their common loyalty to Christ and his way. In the Book of Acts and other New Testament writings, we have snapshots of the nature of their common life (for example, Acts 2:43-47; 4:32-35). In this community the word of God's gracious acts was proclaimed, and the appropriate response was sought. In this community people were baptized into the body of Christ, the church, and received God's grace through the sacraments. In this community the Lord's Supper was celebrated according to Christ's command, "Do this in remembrance of me" (Luke 22:19; 1 Corinthians 11:24-25). So the church today continues as the faithful community hearing the Word of God preached and administering the sacraments.

The major topics of **Article XIV** are purgatory (an intermediate state of punishment and purification where the remaining effects of believers' sins are "purged" so that they may enter heaven), the adoration of images and relics, and the invocation of saints. These ideas and practices, important in Roman Catholicism, are denied as unsupportable by the Scripture.

Article XV is another strongly worded anti-Roman Catholic statement. The Article asserts that it is contrary to the Scriptures to conduct worship in a language that is not understood by the people. In Wesley's time this referred to the Roman Catholic Mass and other services that were conducted in the Latin language which, of course, was the popular language of the ancient Roman Empire. After the fall of Rome and in the ensuing centuries, while the church continued to employ Latin for its liturgy, it fell into disuse among the common people, making it difficult for them to participate fully in worship.

The definition of a sacrament is offered in **Article XVI**. A sacrament is "ordained" (or instituted) by Christ. It is a sign of God's grace by which God works in us to create, strengthen, and confirm our faith. Only two sacraments meet these criteria according to the Article: baptism and the Lord's Supper (or Holy Communion). In addition to these two, the Roman Catholic Church has designated five more: confirmation, penance, marriage, ordination, and extreme unction (now called the anointing of the sick). This Article denies that these five may be called sacraments, although many of us would testify that they may be the bearers of God's grace. There is also a caution that the two sacraments, baptism and the Lord's Supper, were not meant by Christ to be reverenced in and of themselves ("gazed upon" or "carried about") but to be received in faith as gifts of God and means of grace.

The Articles turn next to a closer examination of both baptism and the Lord's Supper. Baptism is the theme of **Article XVII**. We are informed that baptism is a sign of professing the Christian faith that marks us for life as followers of Christ. But, more than that, baptism is also the sign of "regeneration or the new birth." It is a principal means by which the pardoning, forgiving, redeeming, justifying, and life-giving grace of God is conveyed into the life of the person baptized. It marks the beginning of the Christian life. Furthermore, the Article states, the baptism of children, a practice that has ancient roots, is to be retained in the church. This is an important point because some Protestant churches do not baptize infants and young children.

United Methodism has developed an extensive theology of baptism. Its views are officially stated in a document titled "By Water and the Spirit," which was adopted at the 1996 General Conference. The document is worth personal and group study.

The second sacrament, the Lord's Supper, is dealt with in **Article XVIII.** The Lord's Supper is a communal meal in which the followers of Christ gather according to the directions he gave during his earthly ministry. He instructed his disciples to continue to share the bread and cup after his example (Mark 14:22-25; compare 1 Corinthians 11:23-26). Communion, therefore, is "a sign of the love that Christians ought to have among themselves one to another." But it is more. When we receive the elements in the proper spirit and with faith, trusting God's gracious pardon and empowerment in Christ, we are actually receiving the benefits of Jesus' death and resurrection. The Article denies transubstantiation, the Roman Catholic view that in the Lord's Supper the elements of bread and wine substantially become the body and blood of Christ.

We have seen in the earlier chapter on Wesley's sermons that for him the Lord's Supper was an important means of grace. One of the sermons, "The Duty of Constant Communion," urges the Methodist people to receive the Lord's Supper as frequently as possible because it is a vehicle by which God's saving and nurturing grace is conveyed to those who commune in faith.

Articles XIX and **XX** are also related to the Lord's Supper, especially its practice in Roman Catholicism. For many centuries in western Christianity, especially in what became the Roman Catholic Church, only the bread (called the "Host") was offered to laypeople at the Lord's Supper. The Protestant Reformers believed that laypeople should receive both the bread and the wine because Jesus offered both to his disciples. This view is voiced in **Article XIX.** Today in United Methodist, Roman Catholic, and many other churches, both the bread and the cup are offered to those who receive Communion.

Christ's one perfect sacrificial offering for the sins of the human race is announced in **Article XX.** In so doing, the Article denies the Roman Catholic view that in the Mass there is a resacrificing of Christ for human sin. The idea that Christ's sacrifice can be repeated is labeled "a blasphemous fable and dangerous deceit."

The Roman Catholic practice of celibacy and forbidding its priests to marry is the topic of **Article XXI**. Protestants found this unacceptable because, as the Article states, there was no biblical direction that commanded singleness or excluded marriage for the clergy. Methodism has never forbidden its clergy to marry, although Francis Asbury, the first elected Methodist bishop in America, thought that singleness was better for his preachers because unmarried they would be more wholly devoted to their work.

The final Article in this cluster, **Article XXII**, claims the right of churches to "ordain, change, or abolish [their] rites and ceremonies," since they are located in a "diversity of countries, times," and human situations. However, there is a strongly worded indictment of anyone who "through . . . private judgment, willingly and purposely" changes any of the church's rites and ceremonies that are not contrary to Scripture and are commonly accepted by the church. This puts private judgment over the "common order of the church" and endangers the life of its people.

(5) The Christian in Society (Articles XXIII–XXV)

Article XXIII—Of the Rulers of the United States of America
The President, the Congress, the general assemblies, the governors, and the councils of state, *as the delegates of the people*, are the rulers of the United States of America, according to the division of power made to them by the Constitution of the United States and by the constitutions of their respective states. And the said states are a sovereign and independent nation, and ought not to be subject to any foreign jurisdiction.

Article XXIV—Of Christian Men's Goods
The riches and goods of Christians are not common as touching the right, title, and possession of the same, as some do falsely boast. Notwithstanding, every man ought, of such things as he possesseth, liberally to give alms to the poor, according to his ability.

Article XXV—Of a Christian Man's Oath
As we confess that vain and rash swearing is forbidden Christian men by our Lord Jesus Christ and James his apostle, so we judge that the Christian religion doth not prohibit, but that a man may swear when the magistrate requireth, in a cause of faith and charity, so it be done according to the prophet's teaching, in justice, judgment, and truth.

This is a short cluster of three Articles that deal with the relation of Christian believers to the state and society in which they live. The first, **Article XXIII**, was not one of the original Articles sent by Wesley in the

Sunday Service and has no roots in the Anglican Thirty-nine Articles. It was added by the American Methodist preachers to show their loyalty to the government of the United States. We need to remember that in 1784, the United States had been an independent nation for only a few years. It must also be remembered that during the American struggle for independence, Methodists were suspected of disloyalty to the patriot cause. This was largely the result of John Wesley's pamphlet *A Calm Address to Our American Colonies* (1775), in which he urged the colonists to "cool it" with regard to their desire for independence. When the new nation was born, it was altogether proper, the Methodists reasoned, to assert that the national and state governments were proper authorities. Their power should be recognized. Furthermore, these governments should "not . . . be subject to any foreign jurisdiction." Relations between the United States and the parent country remained strained for decades to come, with the War of 1812 being one violent manifestation of this strained relationship.

Article XXIV states the conviction that Christian people possess the right to own private property. However, it is quickly added that those who own property should "liberally . . . give . . . to the poor." Concern for the poor has been a characteristic of Methodism since its earliest days. One of John Wesley's most practical sermons, "The Use of Money" (1760), exhorts the Methodist people to earn all they can, save all they can, and give all they can. One United Methodist bishop has suggested that using Wesley's measuring stick today, most of us are "two-thirds Wesleyans." Christians must be compassionate toward the poor, just as God is always gracious toward them. We have a right to own property; we have an obligation to share what we have with the poor.

The final Article in this set, **Article XXV**, which concerns "swearing," has nothing to do with using "bad words" in the modern sense. It relates to using an oath to confirm a statement or a promise in a way forbidden by Jesus in the Sermon on the Mount (Matthew 5:33-37) and by the writer of the Letter of James (James 5:12). Although the word of a Christian should always be a testimony to the truth and, therefore, trustworthy, this Article gives permission to take an oath before a magistrate when it is required. So, when ordered, we may *"swear* to tell the truth, the whole truth, and nothing but the truth."

We have now finished a discussion of the twenty-five Articles of Religion. However, two unnumbered paragraphs are appended to the Articles in *The Book of Discipline*; and we must pay attention to each of them, even though they are not considered binding doctrinal standards of the denomination. The first originated with The Methodist Protestant

Church, a church that separated from The Methodist Episcopal Church in 1830 and that was a reunion partner with The Methodist Episcopal Church and The Methodist Episcopal Church, South in the creation of The Methodist Church in 1939. This paragraph was taken from the Methodist Protestant *Discipline* and given its present status by the Uniting Conference that formed The Methodist Church in 1939. A note in our present *Discipline* indicates that this paragraph "was not one of the Articles of Religion voted upon by the three churches" that united in 1939. However, its location in the *Discipline* gives it important status. It reads as follows:

Of Sanctification
Sanctification is that renewal of our fallen nature by the Holy Ghost, received through faith in Jesus Christ, whose blood of atonement cleanseth from all sin; whereby we are not only delivered from the guilt of sin, but are washed from its pollution, saved from its power, and are enabled, through grace, to love God with all our hearts and to walk in his holy commandments blameless.

We have noted in the previous chapters that holiness, or sanctification, is an important theme in Wesleyan theology. It is not strange, therefore, that this theme appears with the Articles of Religion. Substantially, it gives a definition of sanctification as the "renewal of our fallen nature by the Holy Ghost" made possible through Jesus' sacrificial death. By grace we are enabled to love God with our whole being and to follow God's will.

The final unnumbered paragraph was also adopted by the Uniting Conference in 1939. According to the accompanying note, it seeks to interpret the intent of **Article XXIII** for United Methodists outside the United States. Its text follows:

Of the Duty of Christians to the Civil Authority
It is the duty of all Christians, and especially of all Christian ministers, to observe and obey the laws and commands of the governing or supreme authority of the country of which they are citizens or subjects or in which they reside, and to use all laudable means to encourage and enjoin obedience to the powers that be.

The substance of this paragraph follows the injunction of Paul in Romans 13:1: "Let every person be subject to the governing authorities." The Disciplinary paragraph, however, does not include the theological rationale that Paul provided. While the paragraph enjoins obedience to the civil authority, it makes no provision for "civil disobedience" when Christians believe the laws of the governing authority are unacceptable in light of their understanding of God's will.

ASSESSMENT

The Articles of Religion are important historical and theological statements of United Methodist belief. For the most part, they come to us directly from John Wesley, who abridged them from the Church of England's Thirty-nine Articles. In the earlier years of American Methodism, the Articles underwent minor editing and the addition of **Article XXIII** regarding the government of the United States.

There are at least two obvious problems with the Articles. The first pertains to their language. The language in which most of the Articles are framed is sixteenth-century English. Frequently, this antiquarian language makes it difficult to read and understand the text. Few of the Articles are stated with complete clarity for today's readers. Regrettably, many people will be discouraged by this language difficulty and will not persevere in reading and studying them. A less important matter is that the Articles are not stated in gender-inclusive language. For example, we are told in **Article VII** that original sin is "the corruption of the nature of every *man*" and a following Article is titled "Of the Justification of *Man*" **(IX)**. While gender-inclusive language was not an issue in previous centuries, we recognize that it is important for us. The Articles address the human situation, which includes both men and women.

Second, the anti-Roman Catholic substance of **Articles XIV, XV, XVI, XVIII, XIX,** and **XX** is problematic not only in light of changes in Roman Catholic theology and practice but also in the context of the ecumenical age in which we currently live. The Articles were originally composed at a time when the level of friction between the Church of England and the Roman Catholic Church was very high. Feelings about these topics remained quite heated during Wesley's life and well into more recent times. We can understand the historical context and importance of these Articles, but we cannot assume that they speak to the circumstances and needs of our day.

In spite of these problems, the Articles of Religion speak to some of the central theological issues in the Christian faith. We arranged them in five groups or clusters, each of which addresses major areas of Christian thought and United Methodist belief.

(1) Who is the one God in whom we believe? The first four Articles attempt to answer this question by affirming the biblical understanding of God as Trinity: Father, Son, and Holy Spirit. These three exist and work as one. We are informed that God is the "maker and preserver of all things." Jesus Christ, in whom were joined complete humanity and divinity, was the perfect sacrifice for our sin and was raised for us. He is our Savior. The Holy Spirit, who lives among us and in us, is the presence of God that flows from the Father and the Son.

(2) The Bible tells the story of the saving acts of the triune God. It is the primary source for understanding and practicing our faith. The Bible includes sixty-six books, thirty-nine of the Old Testament and twenty-seven of the New. The two Testaments, Old and New, ought to be read and studied for the inspiration and direction they bring to our Christian experience. In them we learn about the everlasting life that is offered to us in Christ "who is the *only* Mediator between God" and the human race.

(3) Each and all of us are not the people God intends us to be, apart from God's prevenient and forgiving grace. We have done what God forbids, and we have failed to do what God requires. By God's grace, however, we are accepted and given new life. We respond by "faith-fully" trusting God's grace. We receive God's pardon and a fresh experience of the Spirit. Our further response is the good works (works of mercy) that testify to our new relationship. At any time we are free to "depart from grace given" and to abandon our status as reconciled people. But by God's grace, we may "rise again and amend our lives."

(4) The church is important to our lives. It is the fellowship of our sisters and brothers in which we gather to worship, to hear God's word preached, and to receive the sacraments of baptism and the Lord's Supper. Baptism is a means by which God's saving grace and new birth are conveyed to us. Baptism marks us as Christian disciples. It is the beginning of our journey as Jesus' followers. The Lord's Supper is the communal meal in which we gather in love for God and for one another. When we faithfully receive the bread and the cup at Communion, we are actually receiving the benefits of Christ's sacrificial death and resurrection as well as the replenishing grace of God.

(5) Christians live in a social context. Those of us in the United States recognize our national, state, and local governments with all their imperfections as "delegates of the people." When required, we are privileged to testify in legal proceedings "in justice, judgment, and truth." We have the right to own goods and property. However, we are always under obligation as Christ's people to share what we have with the poor according to the ways in which we have been blessed.

CONCLUSION

The Articles of Religion have had a unique place in Methodist life since they were received by American Methodism in 1784. Founded upon the message of the Bible and the traditional creedal formulations of the church, the Articles are protected by the church's Constitution. They represent a solid basis for the life of The United Methodist Church, especially for its preaching and teaching. The Articles of Religion are certainly worth the patient and persistent study they require.

Some Questions for Reflection and Discussion

(1) Before reading this chapter, did you know anything about the Articles of Religion? Had you ever read and studied them? If you knew nothing about them, why weren't they called to your attention?

(2) Article III speaks about the resurrection of Christ. Why is the resurrection important to Christians?

(3) The Articles, especially Article V and Article VI, remind us that the Old Testament is Scripture for Christians. Why is the Old Testament important? Do you read it regularly? What is the relationship between the Old and New Testaments?

(4) Baptism, one of the two sacraments observed in The United Methodist Church, is spoken about in Article XVII. What does baptism mean to you? Why should infants be baptized? Have you ever participated in a "Congregational Reaffirmation of the Baptismal Covenant," the liturgy for which is found in *The United Methodist Hymnal*? If so, did you find this to be a meaningful experience?

(5) What is the significance of the Lord's Supper for you? How often do you receive it? Should you receive it more frequently? Why or why not?

(6) The anti-Roman Catholic tone of some of the Articles is evident. What do you perceive as the relationship between United Methodists and Roman Catholics? What about our relationship to Eastern Orthodox believers and other Protestants? Should we be engaged in acts of reconciliation with the Roman Catholic Church? Why or why not?

---

(7) What is the duty of a Christian to the civil government? How is our duty changed if a government is clearly speaking or acting in ways that we deem contrary to God's will? Is it ever right for a Christian to engage in acts of "civil disobedience"? Why or why not?

(8) The Articles affirm many of the truths found in the creeds of the Christian church, such as the Apostles' Creed and the Nicene Creed. Do you believe creeds are important? Why or why not? Are creeds used in your church?

SUGGESTIONS FOR FURTHER READING AND STUDY

The Book of Common Prayer. The official Anglican prayerbook that contains the Thirty-nine Articles of the Church of England.

Heitzenrater, Richard P. *Mirror and Memory: Reflections on Early Methodism.* Nashville: Abingdon Press, 1989, 189–204.

Oden, Thomas C. *Doctrinal Standards in the Wesleyan Tradition.* Grand Rapids, MI: Zondervan Publishing House, 1988. Contains a comparison of the Church of England's Thirty-nine Articles and the Methodist Articles in parallel columns. This book also includes important discussions about the nature and substance of Methodist doctrine.

Vogel, Dwight. *By Water and the Spirit: A Study of Baptism for United Methodists.* Nashville: United Methodist Publishing House, 1992. A study guide that includes the statement on baptism adopted by the 1992 General Conference.

---

[1]From "Hymn V," in *Hymns for the Nativity of Our Lord,* by Charles Wesley (The Charles Wesley Society, 1991); pages 13–14.
[2]From *Journal of the 1970 General Conference;* page 25.

Chapter 4
The Confession of Faith of The Evangelical United Brethren Church

The Evangelical United Brethren Church united with The Methodist Church in 1968 to form The United Methodist Church. Regrettably, most United Methodists do not know much about the Evangelical United Brethren (EUB) side of the United Methodist heritage. Even more lamentable is the fact that so few United Methodists, even those from the EUB tradition, are familiar with the fourth doctrinal standard, the Confession of Faith of The EUB Church. In the section that follows, we will discuss the origins of the Confession. This discussion will also involve a brief treatment of the history of The EUB Church.

HISTORICAL BACKGROUND

The EUB Confession is rooted in two early predecessors, the Confession of Faith of the former Church of the United Brethren in Christ (UB), composed as early as 1789, and the Articles of Faith of the former Evangelical Church (EV), which were composed in 1809. These two statements of faith were originally published in German, since both churches at the outset were German speaking.

It is usually assumed that the UB Confession was prepared by Philip William Otterbein (1726–1813), an ordained German Reformed Church pastor and co-founder of the UB with reformed Mennonite Martin Boehm (1725–1812), for use in Otterbein's German Reformed congregation in Baltimore. Otterbein and Boehm collaborated in the founding of the UB in 1800. In 1814, the UB published its rules of discipline and its (Otterbein's) Confession. It included six main paragraphs. These dealt with the triune God (Paragraphs 1–3); the biblical way of salvation through Christ (Paragraphs 4–5); and the "ordinances" of baptism, the Lord's Supper, and footwashing (Paragraph 6). The washing of feet was especially meaningful to people with a Mennonite background.

The first General Conference of the UB in 1815 revised and enlarged the Confession and the following year published it in its first *Discipline*. The new Confession included several changes that strengthened its theological statement. For example, in the first paragraph where it asserts that "God created heaven and earth," the word *triune* was added so that it read the "triune God created heaven and earth."

A few minor alterations to the Confession were made in the 1817 UB *Discipline*. For the next six decades, however, few changes in the document were made. In 1889, the UB General Conference, after considerable debate, approved a new Constitution for the church and an enlarged Confession. A minority of the membership was unhappy with this action and with other trends in the denomination. Led by Bishop Milton Wright (1817–1917), father of Orville and Wilbur Wright of aviation fame, they separated from the UB and formed the Church of the United Brethren in Christ, Old Constitution.

The UB Confession approved in 1889 contained thirteen Articles, compared to the six paragraphs in the earlier *Disciplines*. While the 1889 Confession (and its predecessor) reflects many of the themes that are prominent in the Methodist Articles of Religion, it also represents the influence of the Reformed *Heidelberg Catechism* (1562), the movement known as Reformed Pietism, and some traces of the Anabaptist tradition (of which the Mennonites were part). The Confession is one of the gifts the UB brought to its union with The Evangelical Church in 1946.

The Evangelical Church (EV) was founded by Jacob Albright (1759–1808) in 1807. It was originally known as the *Evangelische Gemeinschaft* (Evangelical Association). Albright's religious background was Lutheran, but he was significantly influenced by the UB and Methodists. Under Albright's leadership the Evangelicals formulated a *Discipline* that was based on the Methodist Episcopal *Discipline* and included the Methodist Articles of Religion. Since Albright's church, like the UB, was German speaking, the EV *Discipline*, including the Methodist Articles, was published in German. They referred to their confessional statement as Articles of Faith.

The EV Articles of Faith reduced the twenty-five Methodist Articles to nineteen. The EV Articles deleted seven Methodist Articles that were anti-Roman Catholic or anti-Anabaptist. The EV Articles then added an Article, "Of the Last Judgment," and an extended essay on "Entire Sanctification" that was appended to the Articles. The EV Articles also included some editorial changes in the Methodist Articles, such as the elimination of technical theological terms, for example, *Pelagians* and *transubstantiation*.

In 1891, the EV suffered a division over theological issues and personal antagonisms. A new denomination, called The United Evangelical Church, was born out of the conflict. While the EV continued to adhere to its traditional Articles of Faith, The United Evangelical Church created new Articles of Faith by accepting the old nineteen and adding six new Articles, bringing theirs to twenty-five Articles. The EV and The United Evangelical Church reunited in 1922 and called themselves The Evangelical Church. The reunified church adopted the earlier nineteen Articles of Faith but included the doctrinal emphases of the United Evangelicals in a later section of their new *Discipline*.

The UB and the EV united in 1946 in Johnstown, Pennsylvania, to form The Evangelical United Brethren Church (EUB). The EUB General Conference authorized the publication of the doctrinal standards of each of the two predecessor denominations, the Confession of Faith (UB) and the Articles of Faith (EV), to be placed side-by-side in their new *Discipline*. In 1958, the General Conference commissioned the EUB Board of Bishops "to conduct a study of the respective confessions of faith of the two former communions, with a view to combining both statements into a unified creedal statement of faith." The new document was to integrate the two doctrinal statements in contemporary language without compromising their content. This task was completed for the 1962 EUB General Conference when the Confession of Faith of The Evangelical United Brethren Church was adopted and placed in its 1963 *Discipline*. When The Evangelical United Brethren Church and The Methodist Church united in 1968, the EUB Confession of Faith was accepted as one of the four doctrinal standards of the new denomination. That Confession represents the theological heritage of both churches that more than twenty years before formed The Evangelical United Brethren Church.

CONTENT

The complete text of the EUB Confession of Faith, like the Methodist Articles of Religion, is printed in *The Book of Discipline of The United Methodist Church*. We have included the entire text of the Confession below, printed in bold type with commentary on each of its Articles. Although the Articles could be grouped in a manner similar to the Methodist Articles of Religion, since there are only sixteen, we will treat each of them separately.

Article I—God
We believe in the one true, holy and living God, Eternal Spirit, who is Creator, Sovereign and Preserver of all things visible and invisible.

He is infinite in power, wisdom, justice, goodness and love, and rules with gracious regard for the well-being and salvation of men, to the glory of his name. We believe the one God reveals himself as the Trinity: Father, Son and Holy Spirit, distinct but inseparable, eternally one in essence and power.

The EUB Confession begins at a place almost identical to that of the Methodist Articles and the great creeds of the Christian church, that is, with belief in God. **Article I** affirms belief in one trinitarian God who creates, preserves, and rules over all things. Of all that claims to be worthy of our loyalty and worship, there is really only one "true, holy and living God" who deserves our praise, faith, and obedience. To worship or serve any other thing or being is to engage in idolatry, the most serious sin described in the Bible. God told the people of Israel, "I am the LORD your God, who brought you out of the land of Egypt, out of the house of slavery; you shall have no other gods before me" (Exodus 20:2).

God is a spiritual being with no beginning and no end, unlimited by space or time. This concept is extremely difficult for many of us to understand, since we are so accustomed to thinking in terms of things that are finite, limited by both time and space.

The Scripture teaches us who God is. God is the Creator. From the earliest chapters of the Bible (Genesis 1–3), we are reminded that it is God who has made the universe and all that is in it (See also Psalm 8 and Isaiah 40:28.). Beyond creating the vastness of the universe, God has also created us and knows us. Addressing God, the psalmist acknowledged:

> For it was you who formed my inward parts;
>   you knit me together in my mother's womb.
> I praise you, for I am fearfully and wonderfully made.
>   (Psalm 139:13-14a)

God is also the Preserver. God's presence sustains the universe and those in it. Israel was kept and protected by God, as was every faithful person in it (Psalm 121). It was God's Holy Spirit who empowered, guided, and guarded the earliest Christian community. That is a principal message of the Book of Acts and the other writings of the New Testament. In the same way God preserves us.

God is the Sovereign. No other person or group of persons, no other power in the universe, has the right, authority, or power to rule. Although other persons or powers challenge God's rule and sometimes appear to overcome God's purpose for us and the world, there is still only one Sovereign whose rule triumphs and whose kingdom is without end. We know this because, as the Article states, there is no limit to God's "power, wisdom, justice, goodness and love." God exercises these graciously for our welfare and salvation.

The last statement in this Article affirms the trinitarian nature of God: "The one God reveals himself as the Trinity: Father, Son and Holy Spirit." We have already noticed that all the other United Methodist doctrinal standards, Wesley's *Notes* and Standard Sermons and the Methodist Articles of Religion, assert that God is to be understood as Trinity. This understanding, of course, is not unique to United Methodism. The trinitarian understanding of God is rooted in the Bible and has been central to the Christian tradition since the earliest centuries of the church. Faith in the trinitarian God is a concept we hold in common with other Protestants, Roman Catholics, and the Eastern Orthodox.

Article II—Jesus Christ

We believe in Jesus Christ, truly God and truly man, in whom the divine and human natures are perfectly and inseparably united. He is the eternal Word made flesh, the only begotten Son of the Father, born of the Virgin Mary by the power of the Holy Spirit. As ministering Servant he lived, suffered and died on the cross. He was buried, rose from the dead and ascended into heaven to be with the Father, from whence he shall return. He is eternal Savior and Mediator, who intercedes for us, and by him all men will be judged.

The second person of the Trinity, Jesus Christ, is the subject of **Article II**. His very name is an important statement of faith. *Jesus* is a Hebrew name that means "Yahweh saves." *Yahweh* is one of the Hebrew names for God. *Christ* comes from the Greek term *Christos*, which is a translation of the Hebrew word *maschiach*, which means "Messiah," or God's "Anointed One." When we speak of Jesus Christ, we are really making a faith statement, namely, that Jesus is the Messiah, the one expected by the people of Israel in biblical times who would deliver God's people and inaugurate a new age in human history. We confess that Jesus is God's "anointed one," not only for us, but for the salvation of the whole world.

We have already noted in the previous chapter that the Christian church struggled for decades with answering the question, "Who is Jesus?" Is Jesus God? Is Jesus human? The church concluded that Jesus was both completely God and completely human. Both divinity and humanity resided "perfectly and inseparably" in him.

Like the Methodist Articles, the EUB Confession refers to Jesus as the enfleshment (incarnation) of the Word. The concept of the word of God is important in the Bible. In Genesis, for example, God speaks the word and Creation occurs (Genesis 1:1–2:4a). The Old Testament prophets were called to address the people of Israel with the word of the Lord. In the New Testament, God's word is declared by Jesus and the earliest Christians. In the Gospel of John, however, Jesus not only announces God's word. He is the Word incarnate. Here are the opening sentences of John's Gospel:

> In the beginning was the Word, and the Word was with God, and the Word was God. He was in the beginning with God. All things came into being through him, and without him not one thing came into being. . . .
> And the Word became flesh and lived among us, and we have seen his glory, the glory as of a father's only son, full of grace and truth.
>
> (John 1:1-3a; 14)

This Article simply reiterates the substance of this biblical idea. Jesus Christ is the Word made flesh. He is God's "only begotten Son." We are also told that Jesus was the child of the virgin Mary by the Holy Spirit (Matthew 1:18-25).

Jesus is identified as "ministering Servant." He is called "servant" in the New Testament (for example, Acts 3:13, 26; 4:27, 30; Philippians 2:7 ["slave"]). The early Christians believed that Jesus was the servant spoken of in such Old Testament passages as Isaiah 42:1-4; 49:1-6; 50:4-9; and especially 52:13–53:12. In quick succession the Article informs us that the "ministering Servant" Jesus "lived, suffered and died on the cross," "was buried, rose from the dead and ascended into heaven to be with the Father." Jesus will return. We say in the United Methodist liturgy for the Lord's Supper, "Christ has died; Christ is risen; Christ will come again." Wisely, there is no speculation in the Article concerning when this return will occur, although many people since, and some now, are willing to use biblical texts to engage in such conjecture. Historically, setting times for the return of Christ has proven to be hazardous. For centuries Christians have developed elaborate chronological schemes to forecast Christ's return. None of them has proved accurate. Jesus warned, "About that day and hour no one knows, neither the angels of heaven, nor the Son, but only the Father" (Matthew 24:36). His return could occur at any time. Therefore, he urged his followers always to be prepared.

Finally, it is forcefully stated that Jesus, the second person of the Trinity, is "eternal Savior and Mediator." As the writer of the Letter to the

Hebrews says, Christ "always lives to make intercession for" us (Hebrews 7:25). He is our representative before God. By him all people will be judged as to their faithfulness in trusting and obeying the triune God.

Article III—The Holy Spirit

We believe in the Holy Spirit who proceeds from and is one in being with the Father and the Son. He convinces the world of sin, of righteousness and of judgment. He leads men through faithful response to the gospel into the fellowship of the Church. He comforts, sustains and empowers the faithful and guides them into all truth.

The third person of the Trinity, the Holy Spirit, is the subject of **Article III.** We are informed that the Holy Spirit proceeds from both the Father and the Son and is one with them. Similar wording is found in the Methodist Articles of Religion. United Methodists share with other Protestants and Roman Catholics the view that the Holy Spirit "proceeds" from *both* the Father and the Son. The Eastern Orthodox Church, however, holds that the Holy Spirit "proceeds" only from the Father. This may not seem to be a matter of great consequence to us, but it has been a serious point of contention between Western and Eastern Christianity and remains a difference.

The pronoun *He* used in this Article reminds us that the Holy Spirit is not the impersonal power or force of God but the very person of God. Therefore, the Holy Spirit should not be referred to as "It." We have said in the previous chapter that the Holy Spirit of God has always existed. The Spirit was deeply involved in the life of the people of Israel in Old Testament times. The Spirit's presence and power were evident in the deeds of Joshua (Deuteronomy 34:9), in the courage of Samson (Judges 14:6), and in the work of the prophets (Isaiah 61:1). The prophet Joel wrote of God's promise that the Spirit of God with accompanying gifts would someday be known and experienced by all people, not just by Israel, in a fresh and dynamic fashion. Joel repeated God's pledge:

> I will pour out my spirit on all flesh;
> your sons and your daughters shall prophesy,
> your old men shall dream dreams,
> and your young men shall see visions.
> (Joel 2:28)

The early Christians believed that this promise was fulfilled fifty days after Easter on the Day of Pentecost. This event is described in the Book of Acts, Chapter 2.

Since the Day of Pentecost, the Holy Spirit has been a renewing and empowering presence among God's people. The EUB Confession is much more helpful in understanding the work of the Spirit than the Methodist Articles because it provides a description of the Spirit's work, which the Methodist statement does not. According to the Confession, the Holy Spirit performs three tasks. First, the Spirit convinces us of the nature and seriousness of our sin. We are not the righteous people God has designed us to be. Our unrighteousness, failing to do what God expects and doing what God forbids, jeopardizes our relationship with God. This failure brings us under God's judgment. At the same time, it prohibits us from enjoying the blessings that attend those who worship and serve God with all they are and have. The Holy Spirit convinces us of our danger as sinful, unrighteous people living under the judgment of God.

Second, the Holy Spirit leads us to recognize the good news of God's forgiving and revitalizing grace. We are moved by the Spirit to a faithful response to God's love by trusting and obeying God. The Spirit also guides us into the fellowship of the church, the body of Christ, the company of those who, like us, recognize their desperate need of divine grace and have surrendered themselves to it.

Third, the Spirit accomplishes a nurturing role. Since Christians are not exempt from torment, grief, and pain, we need the Spirit's comfort. In moments of distress, difficulty, and doubt, the Spirit sustains us. During times of faltering, weakness, and challenge, the Spirit empowers us to be and to do what could not be done without the Spirit. Furthermore, the Spirit teaches us truth and leads us not only to accept it but to do what is both true and right.

Article IV—The Holy Bible

We believe the Holy Bible, Old and New Testaments, reveals the Word of God so far as it is necessary for our salvation. It is to be received through the Holy Spirit as the true rule and guide for faith and practice. Whatever is not revealed in or established by the Holy Scriptures is not to be made an article of faith nor is it to be taught as essential to salvation.

Like the Methodist Articles of Religion, the EUB Confession is clear in stating the nature and authority of the Bible. Both the Methodist and the Evangelical United Brethren traditions historically have not wavered on this issue even though there has been occasional heated discussion in each of the predecessor denominations regarding the interpretation of Scripture.

Article IV affirms belief in the Bible, composed of both Testaments, which "reveals the Word of God" and includes all things "necessary for our salvation." No attempt is made, as in the Methodist Articles, to cite the names of the books of the Old Testament. It is simply assumed that we know that the Bible is composed of sixty-six books (thirty-nine in the Old Testament and twenty-seven in the New). No other document, source, or revelation is required to know and understand the identity of God, our need of God's grace, and the new life God gives to all who are willing to accept it by their faith in the triune God. We know God's word through the biblical message. This certainly includes our knowledge of God through Jesus Christ, who is God's Word and who is known through the text of Scripture.

The Holy Spirit is identified as the One through whom we receive the biblical message and who teaches us that the Scripture is the "true rule and guide for faith and practice." It has long been accepted that the Holy Spirit inspired the writers of the Bible to draft the biblical text. For just as long, it has been established that the Holy Spirit also inspires the readers as they study the text for its message and resolve to apply it to their lives. The Bible, therefore, is the indispensable means by which God teaches us what to believe and what to do.

The final statement in this Article asserts that if an idea or practice "is not revealed in or established by the Holy Scriptures," it does not qualify to be taught by the church "as essential to salvation." In other words, whatever is preached, taught, and practiced by the church as fundamental to our relationship to God and our neighbors must be based in the biblical record.

Article V—The Church

We believe the Christian Church is the community of all true believers under the Lordship of Christ. We believe it is one, holy, apostolic and catholic. It is the redemptive fellowship in which the Word of God is preached by men divinely called, and the sacraments are duly administered according to Christ's own appointment. Under the discipline of the Holy Spirit the Church exists for the maintenance of worship, the edification of believers and the redemption of the world.

To this point the EUB Confession follows the basic pattern of the Methodist Articles. The Confession's **Articles I, II,** and **III** correspond to the first four Methodist Articles (the Triune God); and **Article IV** of the Confession coincides with Methodist **Articles V** and **VI** (Scripture). However, while the Methodist Articles turn next to the matter of sin and salvation followed by church and sacraments, the Confession reverses the order. It deals first with the church and sacraments, then with sin and salvation.

Article V speaks of the church as the whole community of those who truly believe in and trust God and who live under Christ's lordship. This is not a parochial definition of the church. It reminds us that the church encompasses all of every age, race, language, and nation who accept the grace of the triune God and who are committed to be genuine disciples of Jesus. The church is *one*—there is only one body of Christ, which includes all his people (1 Corinthians 12:27). The church is *holy*—a people called and set aside to worship and serve God in all that they are and do (1 Peter 1:15-16). The church is *apostolic*—it accepts and lives by the message Jesus taught his apostles and they in turn have conveyed to us, primarily through the Bible (for example, 1 Corinthians 15:3-11). The church is *catholic*—it is the universal worldwide community of those who accept Jesus as Savior and Lord.

The Article refines the definition of the church by saying that it is the fellowship of those redeemed (set free from their enslavement to sin) by God's grace. In this fellowship God's Word, based in Scripture and Jesus (the Word), is proclaimed by persons (men *and* women) who are called by God for this task. The sacraments, baptism and the Lord's Supper, are regularly and properly administered according to the direction of Christ.

Finally, we are informed that the church exists for three principal reasons: (1) to maintain authentic and faithful worship, (2) to nurture those who belong to its fellowship, and (3) to preach and live the good news of God's love in order that the world might believe and become what God intends it to be.

Article VI—The Sacraments

We believe the Sacraments, ordained by Christ, are symbols and pledges of the Christian's profession and of God's love toward us. They are means of grace by which God works invisibly in us, quickening, strengthening and confirming our faith in him. Two Sacraments are ordained by Christ our Lord, namely Baptism and the Lord's Supper.

We believe Baptism signifies entrance into the household of faith, and is a symbol of repentance and inner cleansing from sin, a representation of the new birth in Christ Jesus and a mark of Christian discipleship.

We believe children are under the atonement of Christ and as heirs of the Kingdom of God are acceptable subjects for Christian Baptism. Children of believing parents through Baptism become the special responsibility of the Church. They should be nurtured and led to per-

sonal acceptance of Christ, and by profession of faith confirm their Baptism.

We believe the Lord's Supper is a representation of our redemption, a memorial of the sufferings and death of Christ, and a token of love and union which Christians have with Christ and with one another. Those who rightly, worthily and in faith eat the broken bread and drink the blessed cup partake of the body and blood of Christ in a spiritual manner until he comes.

According to **Article VI**, there are two sacraments directed by Christ to be administered to his people. They are baptism and the Lord's Supper (Holy Communion). Both are "symbols and pledges" of our faith and of God's grace for us. The sacraments are used by God to enliven, fortify, and ratify our faith in God.

The Article asserts that baptism includes four benefits, all of them interrelated. First, it indicates our initiation into membership in the "household of faith," the church. Baptism is required of all who become full members of the church. Second, baptism is a sign of "repentance and inner cleansing from sin." Although infants cannot make such a promise, young people and adults at the time of baptism are asked if they repent of sin, put their trust in God's grace, and accept the power God gives to resist evil. Third, baptism represents new birth in the life of the believer who receives it. The baptismal liturgy of The United Methodist Church says that through baptism, "we are incorporated into God's mighty acts of salvation and given new birth through water and the Spirit."[1] Fourth, baptism is "a mark of Christian discipleship." When we are baptized, Christ's mark is placed on our lives; and we are committed to live in obedience by his grace from that time forth.

Since children are also the beneficiaries of Christ's atoning death and are heirs to God's kingdom, they are eligible to receive baptism. The statement recalls Jesus' words, "Let the little children come to me, and do not stop them; for it is to such as these that the kingdom of God belongs" (Luke 18:16). Those infants and children whose parents profess faith in Christ are a special gift and responsibility of the church. They must be cared for and led to accept Christ as their Savior and Lord. When these children are able to profess faith themselves as people of Christ, their baptism is confirmed.

The Lord's Supper has four primary meanings. First, it represents our redemption. It embodies our pardon, forgiveness, and reconciliation with God made possible through the sacrificial death of Christ. Second, it is a memorial, an occasion when we gratefully remember the manner in which

Christ suffered and died for us. Third, as we eat and drink together at the Lord's table, we are drawn into a closer bond with Christ and with one another. Fourth, when we faithfully receive the bread and the cup, we are spiritually receiving the benefits of Christ's body and blood until his return.

Article VII—Sin and Free Will

We believe man is fallen from righteousness and, apart from the grace of our Lord Jesus Christ, is destitute of holiness and inclined to evil. Except a man be born again, he cannot see the Kingdom of God. In his own strength, without divine grace, man cannot do good works pleasing and acceptable to God. We believe, however, man influenced and empowered by the Holy Spirit is responsible in freedom to exercise his will for good.

Although **Article VII** does not use the term *original sin*, that is the concept that seems to be set forth at the beginning of the Article. All human beings fail to be the righteous people God intends them to be. The corrective for this situation is God's grace. Without grace (the Wesleys would say God's preventing [prevenient], justifying, and sanctifying grace) we have no holiness and are only inclined to think and do evil. Without divine grace we cannot do what is good, pleasing, and acceptable to God.

The Holy Spirit plays a key role in making it possible for human beings to possess and employ free will and to do good. We should remember the substance of **Article III**. Although that Article does not emphasize the Spirit's role in freeing the human will, it does indicate that the Spirit convinces us of our sin, leads us to a faithful response to the gospel, and guides us into the fellowship of the church. When these three actions are taken together, we can see the critical role the Holy Spirit plays in our relationship to God and to one another.

According to **Article VII**, unless people are born again, they cannot see God's kingdom. This statement is based on the important passage in the Gospel of John. In the notable and fascinating dialogue between Jesus and Nicodemus, Jesus says to him, "Very truly, I tell you, no one can see the kingdom of God without being born from above" (John 3:3). As we have seen, the same emphasis on new birth is made in the theology of the Wesleys. The work of God's grace in us results in new life under the presence and power of the Holy Spirit.

Article VIII—Reconciliation Through Christ

We believe God was in Christ reconciling the world to himself. The offering Christ freely made on the cross is the perfect and sufficient

sacrifice for the sins of the whole world, redeeming man from all sin, so that no other satisfaction is required.

The first sentence of **Article VIII** is almost a direct quote from the New Testament. The apostle Paul wrote, "In Christ God was reconciling the world to himself" (2 Corinthians 5:19). *Reconciliation* is one of those beautiful words in the New Testament. It signifies that estrangement has been set aside and that a new stage in human relationships has been achieved. Whereas the persons in a relationship were previously hostile to one another, now they live in agreement and peace. The sin that characterizes our life is hostility to God. It is refusing to acknowledge God as the only one who deserves our faith, worship, and obedience. God is always at work to repair the relationship broken by sin. Reconciliation is the work of God. God's work in the life, death, and resurrection of Jesus Christ has accomplished reconciliation and has inaugurated not only a new age in the relationship between God and us but also new relationships among us as the people of God.

The Article declares that the sacrifice Christ offered on the cross is totally and perfectly adequate to atone for the sins of the world. Christ is not only the agent of reconciliation, he is also the one person through whom redemption has been accomplished. *Redemption* is a word used in both Testaments of the Bible. It was used in the ancient slave market to describe the act by which the freedom of a slave was purchased. The one who bought the freedom of a slave was called the redeemer. In the Old Testament it was Yahweh (God) who redeemed the people of Israel from their Egyptian bondage. In the New Testament it is God in Christ who performs the act of redemption for us. The writers of the New Testament understood that the reconciling, redeeming, sacrificial death of Christ was entirely adequate for our salvation. Speaking of Jesus, the writer of the Letter to the Hebrews expressed the beneficial finality of his death in the following words: "For it was fitting that we should have such a high priest, holy, blameless, undefiled, separated from sinners, and exalted above the heavens. Unlike the other high priests, he has no need to offer sacrifices day after day, first for his own sins, and then for those of the people; this [Jesus] did once for all when he offered himself" (Hebrews 7:26-27).

Article IX—Justification and Regeneration

We believe we are never accounted righteous before God through our works or merit, but that penitent sinners are justified or accounted righteous before God only by faith in our Lord Jesus Christ.

We believe regeneration is the renewal of man in righteousness

through Jesus Christ, by the power of the Holy Spirit, whereby we are made partakers of the divine nature and experience newness of life. By this new birth the believer becomes reconciled to God and is enabled to serve him with the will and the affections.

We believe, although we have experienced regeneration, it is possible to depart from grace and fall into sin; and we may even then, by the grace of God, be renewed in righteousness.

The message of **Article IX** follows along the same lines as Methodist **Articles IX** and **XII**. The basis for our standing with God is, first of all, not founded on what we do or have done. In both the Old and New Testaments, we are taught that no one's deeds are sufficient to earn God's acceptance (for example, Psalm 143:2; Isaiah 64:6; Acts 13:39; Galatians 2:16). We are considered righteous by God through our faith in Jesus Christ on whose account we are justified and pardoned. This is the "justification by faith" that is celebrated in the Bible and is a centerpiece in Wesley's *Notes*, sermons, and the Articles of Religion.

Concurrent with justification is regeneration or the new birth. The Article expresses this clearly. Regeneration is being made new "in righteousness through Jesus Christ, by the power of the Holy Spirit." It is an experience in which we actually participate in the life of God and are reborn. There are places in the Bible where this reality is described. One of them was written by Paul: "So if anyone is in Christ, there is a new creation: everything old has passed away; see, everything has become new!" (2 Corinthians 5:17). Through this new birth we are reconciled to God. Our will and affections are transformed so that we may serve God with all we are and have.

Christians must always remain vigilant, however. For even after justification and new birth, we may turn away from God and abandon the grace that has made possible our forgiveness and reconciliation. Yet, even when we have renounced God by word and act, we may once again be renewed by divine grace.

Article X—Good Works

We believe good works are the necessary fruits of faith and follow regeneration but they do not have the virtue to remove our sins or to avert divine judgment. We believe good works, pleasing and acceptable to God in Christ, spring from a true and living faith, for through and by them faith is made evident.

While our attitudes, words, and actions are not capable of justifying us and bringing us to new birth, they are the indispensable evidence of our faith. Jesus pointed out the importance of how we act when he said, "Not everyone who says to me, 'Lord, Lord,' will enter the kingdom of heaven, but only the one who does the will of my father in heaven" (Matthew 7:21). The same emphasis is found throughout the Bible. The Old Testament prophet Micah pondered the question about what God wants from us as a sign of our faith. He wrote:

> With what shall I come before the LORD,
>   and bow myself before God on high?
> Shall I come before him with burnt offerings,
>   with calves a year old?
> Will the LORD be pleased with thousands of
>   rams,
>   with ten thousands of rivers of oil?
> Shall I give my firstborn for my transgression,
>   the fruit of my body for the sin of my soul?
> He has told you, O mortal, what is good;
>   and what does the LORD require of you
> but to *do* justice, and to *love* kindness,
>   and to *walk humbly* with your God?
>   (Micah 6:6-8; emphasis added)

There is also the classic passage in the Letter of James, mentioned earlier in this book: "For just as the body without the spirit is dead, so faith without works is also dead" (James 2:26).

Those thoughts, words, and actions that are rooted in genuine lively faith please God. They testify to what God has done, and continues to do, in us. "You will know them by their fruits," Jesus said (Matthew 7:16). Nothing gives greater evidence of our gratitude to God or reveals our deepest faith than the way we live.

Article XI—Sanctification and Christian Perfection

We believe sanctification is the work of God's grace through the Word and the Spirit, by which those who have been born again are cleansed from sin in their thoughts, words and acts, and are enabled to live in accordance with God's will, and to strive for holiness without which no one will see the Lord.

Entire sanctification is a state of perfect love, righteousness and true holiness which every regenerate believer may obtain by being delivered from the power of sin, by loving God with all the heart, soul, mind and strength, and by loving one's neighbor as one's self. Through faith

in Jesus Christ this gracious gift may be received in this life both gradually and instantaneously, and should be sought earnestly by every
child of God.

We believe this experience does not deliver us from the infirmities,
ignorance, and mistakes common to man, nor from the possibilities of
further sin. The Christian must continue on guard against spiritual
pride and seek to gain victory over every temptation to sin. He must
respond wholly to the will of God so that sin will lose its power over
him; and the world, the flesh, and the devil are put under his feet. Thus
he rules over these enemies with watchfulness through the power of
the Holy Spirit.

Sanctification, or holiness, is one of the major emphases of Wesleyan
theology. We have already seen that it is prominent in Wesley's *Notes* and
sermons. **Article XI** is divided into three short sections, each of which discusses an important dimension of sanctification.

The first section is one long sentence. We are informed that sanctification is the consequence of God's grace working in the life of the regener-
ated (born again) Christian believer through the Word (Jesus Christ) and
the Holy Spirit. This labor of God in us yields three major results: (1) We
are thoroughly cleansed from sin in our thoughts, words, and deeds.
(2) We are empowered to live in accordance with God's will for our
lives. (3) We are encouraged and energized to be holy in all that we are
and do. The sentence ends with a New Testament quote; we must pursue
"holiness without which no one will see the Lord" (Hebrews 12:14).

The second section introduces us to the matter of "entire sanctification." This is the goal of sanctification. It is God's grace at work in us to
the end that we are blessed with perfect love; that is, love becomes the
supreme controlling force in our lives. As in the theology of John Wesley,
entire sanctification, or Christian perfection, has two facets. It is (a) loving God with all our heart, soul, mind, and strength (Mark 12:30; compare Deuteronomy 6:5) and (b) loving our neighbor as ourselves (Mark
12:31). This perfect love, a gift of God to be received and nurtured, may
become a reality in this life. Every Christian should seek it. It may come
gradually, or it may be given in an instant.

The third section acknowledges that even entire sanctification does not
insulate us from the problems common to human life or from the possi-
bility of sinning. We must remain alert to pride and temptation. If, by
God's grace, we respond completely to God's will, the Holy Spirit will
lead us to victory over those forces that threaten to undo us and to rob us
of the life God intends each and all of us to have.

XII—The Judgment and the Future State

We believe all men stand under the righteous judgment of Jesus Christ, both now and in the last day. We believe in the resurrection of the dead; the righteous to life eternal and the wicked to endless condemnation.

The idea of God's judgment is grounded in the Bible. In the Old Testament, God is the one who judges all the earth's people with righteousness and truth (Psalm 96:10, 13b). The people of Israel conceived of a "day of the Lord" when God's judgment would be visited on the unrighteous (Isaiah 13:6-13; Amos 5:18). Divine judgment continues as a prominent concept in the New Testament. Jesus spoke about it in the Gospel of Matthew (25:31-46). Furthermore, Jesus is viewed as the one who occupies the office of judge (Acts 17:31; 2 Corinthians 5:10). The church's creeds also speak about the role of Jesus as judge. The Apostles' Creed says that "he shall come to judge the quick and the dead." The Nicene Creed states that

> He will come again in glory
> to judge the living and the dead.

Article XII affirms the biblical and creedal judgment role of Jesus. His judgment is not only reserved for a final "judgment day" but is exercised moment by moment as he measures the depth of our faith and the righteousness of our deeds.

This Article speaks about a final resurrection of the dead. It explicitly asserts that in the final resurrection those who are wicked are subject to "endless condemnation." Those who are judged righteous by their faith and its evidence are raised to eternal life (1 Corinthians 15:12-28).

Article XIII—Public Worship

We believe divine worship is the duty and privilege of man who, in the presence of God, bows in adoration, humility and dedication. We believe divine worship is essential to the life of the Church, and that the assembling of the people of God for such worship is necessary to Christian fellowship and spiritual growth.

We believe the order of public worship need not be the same in all places but may be modified by the church according to circumstances and the needs of men. It should be in a language and form understood by the people, consistent with the Holy Scriptures to the edification of all, and in accordance with the order and *Discipline* of the Church.

Nothing is more important to a Christian and the church than worship. **Article XIII** rightly states that worship is both a duty and a privilege. On the one hand, God expects and requires our worship. On the other hand, the opportunity to sing, pray, hear the Scriptures read and preached, receive the sacraments, and be in fellowship with God and our brothers and sisters is a great blessing. Genuine, faithful worship is essential to the church's life. It is an occasion when we praise God in word and music, confess our sin and seek forgiveness, listen to the good news of grace, and respond to its challenge. In worship we commit ourselves and our possessions to God and receive the grace necessary to be the people God calls us to be, ready to reform society and to spread scriptural holiness where we live and work. All this we do both personally and in the company of family and friends who are also devoted to the triune God.

There are echoes of two Methodist Articles in **Article XIII**. In the second paragraph we are informed that the order, or form, of public worship is not required to be identical everywhere. The order, or form, may be altered to accommodate the circumstances and needs of people in a variety of places and conditions. This follows the line of Methodist **Article XXII**. We are also told that the language and form of the liturgy should be understood by those worshiping (similar to Methodist **Article XV** where it is criticizing the Latin Mass) and that worship should be in harmony with the Bible and the disciplinary order of the church.

Article XIV—The Lord's Day

We believe the Lord's Day is divinely ordained for private and public worship, for rest from unnecessary work, and should be devoted to spiritual improvement, Christian fellowship and service. It is commemorative of our Lord's resurrection and is an emblem of our eternal rest. It is essential to the permanence and growth of the Christian Church, and important to the welfare of the civil community.

The roots of **Article XIV** are found in the Bible. The people of Israel were required by God to keep the seventh day of the week as their sabbath. One of the Ten Commandments reads, "Remember the sabbath day, and keep it holy" (Exodus 20:8; Deuteronomy 5:12). The sabbath was a day of rest; for it was held that God spent six days in creating the heavens, the earth, and all that is in them and rested on the seventh day. God set apart the seventh day and consecrated it as the sabbath (Exodus 20:11). God's people were expected to keep the sabbath as a sacred day in which they celebrated God's creative work and refrained from routine business and entertainment.

Jesus' attitude toward the sabbath was scandalous to many. He healed on the sabbath and taught that "the sabbath was made for humankind, and not humankind for the sabbath" (Mark 2:27). In early Christianity the first day of the week (Sunday) replaced the traditional sabbath (Saturday) as the weekly day of worship. It commemorated the resurrection of Jesus on the first day of the week (for example, John 20:19) and became known as the Lord's day.

This Article asserts that Sunday, the Lord's day, has been ordered by God to be a day for worship, spiritual improvement, Christian fellowship, service for God, and rest. This holy day is critical for the Christian church, since it is an appointed time for Christians to gather for worship, although we know that many Christians may choose another time for their corporate worship. When the sabbath is kept as a sacred day, it also benefits the whole community because it provides necessary rest and relaxation for the populace, even those who are not Christian believers.

Article XV—The Christian and Property

We believe God is the owner of all things and that the individual holding of property is lawful and is a sacred trust under God. Private property is to be used for the manifestation of Christian love and liberality, and to support the Church's mission in the world. All forms of property, whether private, corporate or public, are to be held in solemn trust and used responsibly for human good under the sovereignty of God.

The substance of **Article XV** is stated at the outset. All things are owned by God. We are simply the stewards who are given the responsibility to manage faithfully what belongs to God. There is nothing unlawful about owning property so long as we remember this fact.

Two provisions regarding private property are given: (1) It is a vehicle by which we express Christian love with generosity and sensitivity. Although, as John Wesley believed, property and wealth may be a snare that leads to idolatry and destroys holy living, he held that when rightly used, property and wealth may be a means of blessing by which we can provide for those in need. So, when we have supplied the essentials for ourselves and our families, we receive the gift of giving to the poor what they need to live as God intends. Giving to others blesses us. (2) What we possess also makes it possible for us to support the mission of the church. Our gifts sustain the worship and ministry of our local churches. Our gifts undergird pastoral care, evangelistic outreach, the education and nurture of children and adults, ministries to the poor and homeless, and countless other "works of mercy." Our giving also reaches far beyond our local church and community to make possible ministries to those in prison; medical care; education; help for those suffering from natural disasters; and the preaching of God's good news to the least, the last, and the lost. What we have is not only a source of good *for us* but *for others* as well.

The final sentence in this Article broadens the concern for property beyond that which may be considered private. We acknowledge that "corporate or public" property must also be treated as a trust from God. Corporations and governments are under the same mandate as individuals. Corporations and governments are responsible to use what they have and manage for the good of the human race under the sovereignty of God.

Article XVI—Civil Government

We believe civil government derives its just powers from the sovereign God. As Christians we recognize the governments under whose protection we reside and believe such governments should be based on, and be responsible for, the recognition of human rights under God. We believe war and bloodshed are contrary to the gospel and spirit of Christ. We believe it is the duty of Christian citizens to give moral strength and purpose to their respective governments through sober, righteous and godly living.

The opening statement of **Article XVI** is reminiscent of the words of the apostle Paul: "Let every person be subject to the governing authorities; for there is no authority except from God, and those authorities that exist have been instituted by God" (Romans 13:1). It is important to note that the Article states that the civil government's "just powers" derive from God. This seems to imply that a government may exercise "unjust powers" and that these *do not* come from God.

We are counseled to acknowledge the governments under which we live and that provide for our protection. However, these governments bear enormous responsibility. They are based upon and accountable for "human rights under God." According to the Declaration of Independence of the United States of America, these human rights include "life, liberty, and the pursuit of happiness." Every human being in this nation has a just claim to these rights. We may wish to restate this fact by saying that all people have the right to become who God wants them to be. A basic function of government is to bring this fact to reality.

Take note of the strong statement that "war and bloodshed" violate the Christian gospel. Although The United Methodist Church is not a pacifist denomination, its "Social Principles" are clear on the matter of war. "We believe war is incompatible with the teachings and example of Christ. We therefore reject war as an instrument of national foreign policy and insist that the first moral duty of all nations is to resolve by peaceful means every dispute that arises between or among them" (*Book of Discipline*; Para. 69).

Finally, Christians are reminded that the way they live gives "moral strength and purpose" (**Article XVI**) to their governments. By their thoughts, words, and acts, Christians may "reform the nation, particularly the church; ... and ... spread scriptural holiness over the land."[2]

ASSESSMENT

The Confession of Faith of The Evangelical United Brethren Church had a relatively short life in that denomination. It was adopted in 1962, and only six years later the Evangelical United Brethren united with The Methodist Church. We must not forget, however, that the content of the Confession of Faith has roots in predecessor statements of faith in both the United Brethren and Evangelical traditions. Those doctrinal pronouncements have a much longer history.

We can make several comments about the value of the EUB Confession. First, its language is more modern than any of the other three doctrinal standards of the denomination, all of which had their origins in the eighteenth century. The more contemporary prose of the Confession thus enables us to read and understand it more easily than the older three standards. That is certainly an advantage. However, one of the evident flaws in the Confession is the absence of gender-inclusive language. It speaks about the "salvation of *men*" (**Article I**), the Holy Spirit's leading "*men* through faithful response to the gospel" (**Article III**), and all "*men* stand[ing] under the righteous judgment of Jesus Christ" (**Article XII**). This language, of course, is meant to be inclusive. Nevertheless, the Confession's gender-exclusive language is a stumbling block to many.

Second, it should be evident from the text and commentary of each of the Confession's sixteen Articles that they are based in Scripture and are consonant with the major creeds of the church. United Methodism claims that its theology is based primarily in the Bible and that it takes seriously the tradition of the church. The scriptural and traditional foundation of the Articles testifies that is true with the Confession of Faith.

Third, while the content of the Confession does not exhaust the riches of Christian doctrine, it does manage to lay before us the essentials. No statement of faith or creed includes everything that is important. The Confession of Faith, however, sets out the basic elements of the Christian faith in a clear and forceful manner.

CONCLUSION

The Confession of Faith keeps us in touch with another important source of our United Methodist theological heritage. It is a gift to us from our Evangelical United Brethren tradition. Reflected in it are the Methodist Articles of Religion that were so important to The Articles of Faith of The Evangelical Church. The older United Brethren Confession of Faith also reveals the influence of other European theological currents (the Protestant Reformation of the sixteenth century and the seventeenth century movement known as Pietism). When the Evangelical and the United Brethren documents were used to compose the EUB Confession of Faith, they each contributed to a document that continues to serve our church.

Some Questions for Reflection and Discussion

(1) Before reading this chapter, did you know anything about the Confession of Faith of The Evangelical United Brethren Church? Had you ever read it?

(2) The Confession speaks about Jesus' humanity and divinity "perfectly and inseparably united." Have you thought about this and what it means? Is this union important? Why or why not?

(3) Wesley's *Notes*, sermons, the Articles of Religion, and the Confession all indicate the importance of Jesus' death as more than the execution of a martyr. What do you believe to be the significance of Jesus' death? What do the Bible, the creeds, and the doctrinal standards teach about the meaning of the cross and resurrection?

(4) Article X speaks about the importance of "good works." What are "good works," and why are they important?

(5) Wesleyan theology emphasizes "entire sanctification" (for example, see **Article XI**). It is defined as "a state of perfect love" in which we are "delivered from the power of sin." What do you think this means? Why should we seek it?

(6) Do you believe that we all stand under the judgment of God? What does this mean to you?

---

(7) What is worship? Why is worship important? Would you agree with some who say that it is better to feed the poor and to shelter the homeless than to engage in worship? Why or why not?

(8) What do you think about **Article XV**, which deals with the Christian and property? Do you agree that "God is the owner of all things"? What about the statements regarding the use of private property? How do we support the mission of the church through the use of private property?

SUGGESTIONS FOR FURTHER READING AND STUDY

Behney, J. Bruce and Paul H. Eller. *The History of the Evangelical United Brethren Church.* Nashville: Abingdon Press, 1979. Provides a comprehensive survey history of The EUB Church.

O'Malley, J. Steven. "The Distinctive Witness of the Evangelical United Brethren Confession of Faith in Comparison with the Methodist Articles of Religion." Dennis M. Campbell, William B. Lawrence, and Russell E. Richey, eds. *Doctrines and Discipline.* United Methodism and American Culture Series. Nashville: Abingdon Press, 1999. Pages 55–76. Offers an excellent review of the history and substance of the EUB Confession.

---

[1] From "The Baptismal Covenant I," in *The United Methodist Hymnal* (Copyright © 1989 The United Methodist Publishing House); page 33.
[2] From *The Works of John Wesley*, Vol. VIII (Baker Book House, 1979); page 299.

CONCLUSION

$\mathbf{W}$e have now concluded our brief introductory examination of the four official doctrinal standards of The United Methodist Church. Several points need to be made as we complete this study. They include: (1) general comments regarding the standards, (2) a brief review of the main content of the standards, (3) the place of the Disciplinary document "Our Theological Task" in relation to the standards, and (4) a final statement regarding their importance.

GENERAL COMMENTS

The four doctrinal standards are landmark documents in our denominational life. We have attempted to describe the historical background of each of them. As we have said, three of them owe their place to John Wesley. The fourth was formulated by The Evangelical United Brethren Church. There is little debate about their historical significance for our church. There is considerably more debate in some quarters about how binding they should be for United Methodism as it enters a new century. In other words, are the doctrinal standards merely "landmark documents" of historical importance, or are they documents that not only possess historical value but also continue to set forth the basic doctrines of United Methodism?

The doctrinal standards are the only official doctrinal statements of the denomination. Their significance is underscored by their listing in Part II of *The Book of Discipline of The United Methodist Church*, a prominent section at the front of the *Discipline* following the "Historical Statement," which gives a summary of United Methodism, and the church's Constitution. The full texts of the Articles of Religion and the Confession of Faith of The Evangelical United Brethren Church are included in Part II while the *Explanatory Notes Upon the New Testament* and the sermons are simply mentioned in this section.

Each of the standards was believed by its author(s) to be based upon biblical truth and to be faithful to the best tradition of the Christian church, especially its major ecumenical creeds. John Wesley was certainly convinced that his *Explanatory Notes Upon the New Testament* and published sermons were founded in the Bible and thoroughly compatible with the church's tradition. He was likewise persuaded that the Articles of Religion he sent to America contained statements that were consistent with Scripture and with the church's longstanding creeds. The Evangelical United Brethren Confession of Faith was endorsed by its writers as a document rooted in the Bible and in the church's widely accepted creedal positions.

Finally, according to the United Methodist *Book of Discipline*, it appears that the doctrinal standards are meant to be taken seriously. They are not simply to be given a passing nod or to be treated merely as historically interesting. Those who are ordained into the church's ministry are required to study and accept the church's doctrines. We have also mentioned that disseminating "doctrines contrary to the established standards of the Church" (*Book of Discipline*; Para. 2624.1f) is an offense for which pastoral leaders may be officially charged and lose their status, although this happens infrequently.

CONTENT OF THE DOCTRINAL STANDARDS

John Wesley once wrote, "As to all opinions which do not strike at the root of Christianity we 'think and let think'."[1] This is a permissive statement. It does require us, however, to determine what is at the "root of Christianity." It appears that the doctrinal standards state that the following are central to the Christian faith, teachings we share with Christians in other denominations:

(1) The Authority of the Bible

All four standards place great emphasis on the Bible as the primary source from which we draw our understanding and practice of the Christian faith. As the Confession of Faith says, the Bible is "the true rule and guide for faith and practice" (*Book of Discipline*; Para. 62). The Methodist Articles state that whatever is not read in, or proved by, the biblical text is not to be considered an "article of faith" or thought necessary for salvation. Some persons, usually members of quite conservative churches, accuse United Methodists of ignoring the Bible. Regrettably, some United Methodists, at their spiritual peril, do neglect reading and studying the Scripture. However, the official position of the church requires that the Bible be placed in a primary place when we are dealing with our personal and church life.

(2) The Triune God

We believe in one God who is known in three persons: Father, Son, and Holy Spirit. This teaching is based in Scripture and confirmed by the tradition of the Christian church. The doctrinal standards make this belief clear, and we have attempted to show their unanimous affirmation of the triune God. Our prayers, hymns, orders of worship, and daily lives reflect our faith in the trinitarian God whose children we are.

(3) Human Nature and Salvation

All of us stand in need of the grace of the triune God. There is a great disparity in each of us between what God intends us to be and what we really are. We do what God forbids and fail to do what God demands. We fail to worship and serve the God who has made us. Our words and deeds cause pain in the lives of others, even those whom we love most. The Bible describes this condition as sin and warns us that we must respond to God's grace by changing the direction of our lives, receiving God's forgiveness, and being renewed by God's presence and gifts. Jesus Christ, the second person of the Trinity, is critical to a reconciled relationship with God. His sacrificial, atoning death and his resurrection are key events in our pardon and new standing with God. The doctrinal standards affirm Jesus as the only Savior of the world. All people are invited to respond to God's offer of salvation in Christ. By God's prevenient grace, all are able to answer this divine summons.

(4) The Holy Life

We who by faith accept God's forgiving and reconciling grace are expected to grow in grace. We accept God's rule and direction for our lives. We earnestly seek to be and do what God wants. We live moral lives in response to God's grace and following God's commandments. We use the gifts of the Spirit and the means of grace (prayer, Bible study, fasting, Christian fellowship, the Lord's Supper, public worship) for nurture and encouragement along the journey of the faithful life. We engage unselfishly in "works of mercy" or ministry to others. We are representatives of the triune God as the people of Christ. Our goal is to love God with all our heart, mind, soul, and strength and our neighbors as ourselves. We do this by the grace of God.

(5) Church and Sacraments

The church is not unimportant for Christians and the world in which we live. It is the fellowship of Christ's people around the world who have been invited to answer his call to follow him; to love, worship, and serve the triune God; and to love their neighbors as themselves. The church includes all of whatever race, nation, language, or economic class who are committed to Christ as Savior and Lord of their lives. The sacraments of baptism and the Lord's Supper are administered through the church as means by which God's prevenient, justifying, and sanctifying grace is made available to all who are willing to receive it.

"OUR THEOLOGICAL TASK"

In *The Book of Discipline of The United Methodist Church*, immediately following the section on doctrinal standards, is an important document titled "Our Theological Task." This document was originally developed for the 1972 General Conference of The United Methodist Church and was revised by the 1988 General Conference. It is best known for its identification of the so-called "Wesleyan Quadrilateral," which urges the employment of Scripture, tradition, experience, and reason as the four principal sources for thinking "critically on our biblical and theological inheritance, [and] striving to express faithfully the witness we make in our own time" (*Book of Discipline*; Para. 63). Among the four sources, Scripture is identified as "primary."

"Our Theological Task" is worthy of personal and group study. It emphasizes the importance of careful and thoughtful theological reflection for every Christian and for the church. At its outset this document defines theology and speaks about the relationship between "our theological task" and doctrinal standards:

> Theology is our effort to reflect upon God's gracious action in our lives. In response to the love of Christ, we desire to be drawn into a deeper relationship with the "author and perfecter of our faith." Our theological explorations seek to give expression to the mysterious reality of God's presence, peace, and power in the world. By so doing, we attempt to articulate more clearly our understanding of the divine-human encounter and are thereby more fully prepared to participate in God's work in the world.
>
> The theological task, though related to the Church's doctrinal expressions, serves a different function. Our doctrinal affirmations assist us in the discernment of Christian truth in ever-changing contexts. Our theological task includes the testing, renewal, elaboration, and application of our doctrinal perspective in carrying out our calling "to spread scriptural holiness over these lands." (*Book of Discipline*; Para. 63)

"Our Theological Task" distinguishes theology from our doctrinal standards. According to the document, theology and our doctrinal standards serve different functions. While doctrinal standards remain at the center of our church's understanding of the Christian faith, theology involves the way in which we test, renew, elaborate, and apply our doctrinal teachings in a world that is constantly changing. One way of viewing this is to understand a dynamic relationship between our doctrinal standards and "our theological task." The doctrinal standards form the boundaries within which our theologizing takes place. The document reminds us, however, that there is also a place for our theologizing to analyze, interpret, and apply our official doctrinal statements.

Correct Doctrine Important but Not Sufficient

The United Methodist tradition is quite clear that holding all the correct doctrinal ideas is not sufficient to make a Christian. In his sermon "The Way to the Kingdom," John Wesley offered this comment:

> For neither does religion consist in *orthodoxy* or *right opinions*; which, although they are not properly outward things, are not in the heart, but the understanding. A man may be orthodox in every point; he may not only espouse right opinions, but zealously defend them against all opposers; he may think justly concerning the incarnation of our Lord, concerning the ever blessed Trinity, and every other doctrine contained in the oracles of God. He may assent to all . . . three creeds—that called the Apostles', the Nicene, and the Athanasian—yet 'tis possible he may have no religion at all. . . . He may be almost as orthodox as the devil . . . and may all the while be as great a stranger as he to the religion of the heart. ("The Way to the Kingdom," *Works*; Vol. 1, pages 220–21)

Here Wesley was not displaying indifference to sound doctrine. In other places he spoke about believers being committed to the main doctrines of the Christian faith. Sound doctrine is important. It is not enough, however. Religion of the head must be united with religion of the heart. Correct doctrine joined with genuine love for God and neighbor lead us to be who God wants. That is what Wesley meant when he spoke about "practical religion," religion that is practiced. Doctrine forms the basis for our understanding and response to the triune God. There must be a constant link between doctrine and living. Experience cannot be disconnected from our doctrinal standards.

Toward the close of his life, Wesley wrote this often quoted statement that remains provocative:

I am not afraid that the people called Methodists should ever cease to exist either in Europe or America. But I am afraid lest they should only exist as a dead sect, having the form of religion without the power. And this undoubtedly will be the case unless they hold fast both the doctrine, spirit, and discipline with which they first set out.[2]

United Methodists are called on to embrace sound doctrine; to live in the spirit of God's love (loving God and our neighbors in response); and to be God's disciplined people in our thoughts, words, and acts. Our doctrinal standards teach us along this journey.

Some Questions for Reflection and Discussion

(1) What have you learned in this study about the doctrinal standards of The United Methodist Church? In what ways do they help you personally? What place should they have in the life of our denomination?

(2) Do you consider the Bible the "primary" source of what you believe and do? In what ways does the Bible inform your faith?

(3) We have spoken about Jesus' "sacrificial, atoning death." Is this the way you think about the significance of Jesus' death?

(4) The United Methodist tradition has always emphasized holiness and sanctification. Living a holy life is our response to God's forgiving, healing, and renewing grace. In what ways do you and your church exhibit holiness?

(5) Have you read "Our Theological Task," the document mentioned above and which is found in *The Book of Discipline of The United Methodist Church*? If not, ask someone who has a copy to allow you to borrow it. It is fully worth your reading and study. What do you see as the relationship between this document and the doctrinal standards?

(6) It is widely agreed that correct doctrinal ideas are not sufficient for living the Christian life. What is their proper role in your life and in the life of the church?

---

[1] From *The Character of a Methodist*, in *The Works of John Wesley*, Vol. 9, edited by Rupert E. Davies (Abingdon Press, 1989); page 34.

[2] From *Thoughts Upon Methodism*, in *The Works of John Wesley*, Vol. 9, edited by Rupert E. Davies (Abingdon Press, 1989); page 527).

GLOSSARY

Albright, Jacob (1759–1808)—Evangelical preacher, founder, and first bishop of the Evangelical Association, later called The Evangelical Church.

Anglican Church—The Church of England, which was formed in the sixteenth century under King Henry VIII and Queen Elizabeth I. John and Charles Wesley were ordained priests in the Church of England.

Articles of Religion—One of the four doctrinal standards of The United Methodist Church. The Methodist Articles were a revision of the Church of England's Thirty-nine Articles. John Wesley sent his revision of twenty-four Articles to America in 1784.

Atonement—Refers to the death of Jesus on the cross as a sacrifice for human sin.

Baptism—One of the two sacraments of The United Methodist Church. The baptism of infants, youth, and adults is administered in United Methodism. Baptism may be administered by sprinkling, pouring, or immersion. It is a means of conveying God's grace to the recipient and is required before someone unites with the church.

Boehm, Martin (1725–1812)—Mennonite preacher, co-founder and co-bishop with Philip William Otterbein of the Church of the United Brethren in Christ.

Book of Common Prayer—The official prayerbook of the Church of England. It was used extensively by John Wesley. He sent a revised version to American Methodism titled *The Sunday Service of the Methodists in North America* in 1784.

Book of Discipline—Outlines the law, doctrine, administration, and organization of The United Methodist Church. It lists the four doctrinal standards of the denomination. The *Discipline* may be revised by the General Conference, which meets every four years.

Church of England—See Anglican Church above.

Church of the United Brethren in Christ—Founded by Philip William Otterbein and Martin Boehm in 1800. It united with The Evangelical Church in 1946 to form The Evangelical United Brethren Church.

Doctrinal Standards—Four official doctrinal statements of The United Methodist Church that are mentioned in *The Book of Discipline.*

Evangelical Church—Founded by Jacob Albright in 1807. It united with the Church of the United Brethren in Christ in 1946 to form The Evangelical United Brethren Church.

Evangelical United Brethren Church—Formed in 1946 by a union of the Church of the United Brethren in Christ and The Evangelical Church. It united with The Methodist Church in 1968 to form The United Methodist Church.

Holiness—A key concept in Wesleyan theology. It is based on the biblical idea of a life filled with the grace of God devoted to love of God and neighbor. According to Wesley, holiness is the goal of the Christian life.

Holy Spirit—The third person of the Holy Trinity. The Holy Spirit occupies a central role in the salvation and sanctification of the Christian believer and the believing community.

Justification by faith—God's pardoning and accepting love made available through belief in the life, death, and resurrection of Jesus.

Lord's Supper—One of the two sacraments administered in The United Methodist Church. It is a principal means by which God's grace is conveyed into the lives of those who faithfully receive it through the sharing of bread and the cup.

Means of grace—Gifts of God for deepening our holiness. They include Scripture, prayer, fasting, Christian conference, worship, and the Lord's Supper.

Methodist—The name given to one of the groups centrally involved in the eighteenth-century English evangelical revival. The name eventually became associated with that group of people who acknowledged John and Charles Wesley as their leaders.

New birth—The work of God's grace in us that results in new life lived in the presence and with the power of the Holy Spirit.

Otterbein, Philip William (1726–1813)—German Reformed pastor, co-founder and co-bishop with Martin Boehm of the Church of the United Brethren in Christ.

"Our Theological Task"—Important document in *The Book of Discipline of The United Methodist Church* that encourages United Methodists to think and live using four major gifts: Scripture, tradition, reason, and experience.

Pietism—Movement in the seventeenth and eighteenth centuries that emphasized personal religious experience based in prayer, contemplation, Bible study, fellowship with other Christians, and ministry to others.

Prevenient grace—Literally the grace that "comes before." It is God's grace that is "free in all and free for all." This grace makes it possible for everyone to respond to God's offer of forgiving, renewing, and sanctifying grace.

Sacraments—Means by which God's saving, renewing, and nurturing grace is conveyed into the lives of those who appropriately receive them. The two sacraments in United Methodism are baptism and the Lord's Supper.

Sanctification—A biblical word that deals with "holiness of heart and life," a key Wesleyan phrase. See Holiness above.

Sin—The deepest problem in human nature. It is a state in which we live resistant and opposed to worshiping and serving God.

Trinity—The understanding that the one God is known in three persons, Father, Son, and Holy Spirit.

Wesley, Charles (1707–1788)—a co-founder of Methodism with his brother John and hymn writer for Methodism.

Wesley, John (1703–1791)—principal founder of Methodism. Wesley was a priest in the Church of England. His *Explanatory Notes Upon the New Testament*, Standard Sermons, and the Articles of Religion he sent to America are three of the denomination's four doctrinal standards.

Works of mercy—Phrase used by John Wesley to describe the deeds that are done by those truly committed to Jesus Christ. These are essential to the holy life.

Works of piety—Phrase used by John Wesley to describe means of grace used by faithful Christians. They are essential to holy living.

STUDY GUIDE

SESSION ONE

GOALS

To explore why doctrine is important
To explore the relationship between doctrine and the Christian life

MATERIALS

copies of BELIEF MATTERS (one for each person in the group)
copies of *The Book of Discipline of The United Methodist Church*

GETTING INTO THE SESSION

Ask each person to select a partner (the person in the room whom they know least well). The partners should then tell each other why they are in this study group, what their expectations are, and what they want to discover in this study. In the process, they will begin to know each other as persons. Then ask each pair to find another pair, at least one of whom they do not know well, and to repeat the process.

When this exercise has been completed, ask: *What are you willing to do to help fulfill your own expectations?*

Distribute copies of BELIEF MATTERS, along with blank name tags. Ask each person to fill out a tag and to wear it for the rest of the session.

Ask: *Who has heard statements like this: "You can believe anything and be a United Methodist"?*

Is doctrine important? Why or why not? What does "doctrine" mean? What is the relationship between doctrine and the Christian life? (See Introduction, pages 10–11.)

WORKING THROUGH THE SESSION

1. Invite persons to browse through the book to see what headings or sentences catch their eye. Ask for responses, and list these on a chalkboard or on a large piece of paper.

Ask: *Why did these particular headings catch your eye? What about them makes you curious? What about them leads you to say, "I didn't know that!"?*

2. Tell the group that, for United Methodists, doctrine is important—so important that we have doctrinal standards. Using material found in the Introduction to BELIEF MATTERS (pages 9–13), explain what our doctrinal standards are and why we have them. Note that there is some disagreement about whether all the resources that the writer identifies as doctrinal standards are universally accepted as such. However, all four are still important sources for doctrinal understanding in The United Methodist Church. Point out the obvious: This study is about the doctrines defined by those standards.

The fact that we have doctrinal standards does not mean that we cannot deal with new ideas. None of the doctrinal standards, for example, could have anticipated issues raised by the theory of general relativity or by mapping the human genome or by quantum mechanics or by evolution. Having doctrinal standards does mean, however, that we have a solid doctrinal base for our teaching and practice. We have amazing freedom to decide how the standards apply to new situations and ideas. Nevertheless, we do not have the freedom to change what the standards are.

Point out the sections "Doctrinal Standards in American Methodism," "Doctrinal Traditions in The Evangelical Church and The United Brethren Church," and "Doctrinal Standards in The United Methodist Church" in *The Book of Discipline* (pages 50–62). Tell the group that these sections describe the importance of doctrine and of doctrinal standards throughout our history. Arrange for persons who would like to read that material to borrow a copy of *The Book of Discipline*. Perhaps one or more persons would like to report to the group on what they read.

3. On page 20 in BELIEF MATTERS, there is the following quotation from John Wesley: "My intention is, to make them think, and assist them in thinking." Ask: *In light of Wesley's statement, how do you see the importance of thinking in the Christian life?*

CLOSING THE SESSION

Ask persons to read Chapter 1, "John Wesley's *Explanatory Notes Upon the New Testament*," in preparation for the next session.

Close with prayer for understanding and enthusiasm about doctrine.

SESSION TWO

GOALS

To discover Wesley's *Explanatory Notes Upon the New Testament*
To explore core doctrine in the *Notes*
To evaluate the *Notes* as a resource for our faith today

MATERIALS

copies of BELIEF MATTERS
a copy of *Explanatory Notes* if available (See the web site http://Wesley.nnu.edu. Since the web site contains the complete text of the *Notes*, you may want to print out a few pages for illustrative purposes.)
copies of *The United Methodist Hymnal*

GETTING INTO THE SESSION

Ask: *What insights, ah-ha's, or questions do you have from reading Chapter 1 of BELIEF MATTERS?* List responses on a chalkboard or on a large piece of paper. If there are questions you do not know how to answer, tell the group so and make a commitment to find answers. Perhaps you can invite the pastor or someone who has studied Wesley to come in and answer questions during a later session.

Remind the group that Wesley wanted Methodists to think about the Bible and to respond to its message. Ask: *From what you have read about the* **Explanatory Notes**, *do you think they would be helpful in thinking about the Bible?* Distribute copies of the printout from the notes if available. OR, if you can, call up the web site on a computer for people to see.

WORKING THROUGH THE SESSION

1. Comment on the historical background of the *Notes*, particularly what Dr. Yrigoyen calls the four purposes (pages 20–22).

Point out that there are three doctrinal themes lifted up from the *Notes*: sin, salvation, and holiness. Ask: *What does Wesley say about each? Does your thinking on these questions match up with his?*

2. Look at each of the three doctrines separately, using the hymns Dr. Yrigoyen includes in the text. Ask: *What does the hymn say about the doctrine of sin, salvation, and so forth? What other issues does the hymn raise? For example, the hymn "Sinners, Turn, Why Will You Die?"*

assumes the reality of free will. Can we really turn our backs on God and "slight his grace"? What do you think?

3. In dealing with salvation, Dr. Yrigoyen also raises questions about the Trinity and the nature of Christ. Ask: *Why are those important for salvation? Why is free will important? Did Wesley believe in universal salvation? Do you?*

How can salvation be Jesus' work and, at the same time, be the work of the Father and the Spirit?

Why is it important for our understanding of Jesus and of salvation to speak of him as prophet, priest, and king? Was the idea of "prevenient grace" a new one for you? Are you clear on what it means? on why it is important?

4. Holiness, or sanctification, is a hard concept to understand. Look at the definition on page 31. Ask: *How can finite humans expect to live that way? Why is money such an issue in talking about holiness? How are "works of piety" and "works of mercy" gifts from God that help lead us to a life of holiness?*

CLOSING THE SESSION

Summarize by pointing out three important lessons for United Methodists (pages 37–38). Talk about some of the ways that Wesley's comments *cannot* be used today.

Assign Chapter 2 for reading for next time. Remind the group to read and to think about the questions at the end of the chapter.

Ask for volunteers who would be willing to read one of Wesley's sermons and to report to the group on their reading—specifically, what doctrine is the sermon about, and what does the sermon say about that doctrine? See "Suggestions for Further Reading and Study" on page 70 for a list of books containing Wesley's sermons. Remind the readers that when Wesley printed his sermons, he left out nearly all his illustrations, so what they have is the core teaching of the sermon.

Close with prayer.

SESSION THREE

GOALS

To discover Wesley's *Standard Sermons*
To explore what the sermons say about doctrine
To assess the value of the *Standard Sermons* for our time

MATERIALS

copies of BELIEF MATTERS
one or more copies of Wesley's *Standard Sermons* if available

GETTING INTO THE SESSION

1. Comment briefly on the historical background of Wesley's preaching and of the *Standard Sermons* (pages 43–45 of BELIEF MATTERS).

2. Invite the volunteers who read a Wesley sermon to report on their reading. If their report does not specifically identify the doctrine covered in the sermon, ask what doctrine it was and what the sermon said about it. Say: *Remember that Wesley's audience was often composed of people who were uneducated, even illiterate. Why, do you suppose, did these sermons lead so many of them to faith in Christ?*

WORKING THROUGH THE SESSION

1. Ask: *How many core doctrinal themes did we find in the* **Explanatory Notes?** *How many did we discover in this chapter?* (List the themes from both sources in parallel columns on a chalkboard or large piece of paper.) *Can you think of a way to account for the differences?*

Say: "Let's look at some of the specific doctrinal themes. Anyone who read a sermon should feel free to add insights at any time."

2. Ask: *Threefold grace is an important Wesleyan theme. How did Wesley define "grace"? What is "prevenient grace"? How does it work in human life? Have you been aware of this kind of grace in your life? If so, when?*

3. Ask: *The new birth is closely related to justification by faith. How does Wesley define "justification"? How does he define "new birth"? How did Wesley compare new birth to the birth of a child? What are the scriptural marks of the new birth?*

4. Ask: *We have sung "Blessed Assurance" many times. But what is assurance, in Wesley's view? What do you think it means for us?* Remind the group that Wesley once believed that no one had really been born again unless she or he had full assurance, but he later changed that and said assurance was a great gift but not everyone necessarily received it.

5. Ask: *What is "holiness," in Wesley's view? Does that seem to you to be an important goal for the Christian life? What is the connection between holiness and "works of piety"? What did Wesley define as works of piety? Are they important tools for your Christian life? Why or why not?*

6. Remind the group that there was a time in our history when everyone talked about heaven and longing to be there. Today, we hardly hear heaven mentioned, except at funerals. Ask: *What did Wesley have to say about heaven? about the way to get there?*

7. Wesley believed it was hard to be Christians by ourselves. In fact, he once said, "The New Testament knows no solitary religion." Ask: *What do you think? Is it important to be an active member of the church in order to be a Christian? What are the advantages of that? the disadvantages? What do we gain from Christian community? How do we contribute to Christian community?*

CLOSING THE SESSION

Ask: *Since Wesley wrote these sermons over 200 years ago, how are they still valuable for us today? What could we gain from them?* (See pages 67–69.) *How important do you think preaching is for the life of the church today? What do you gain from listening to sermons?*

Remind the group that the next two sessions will cover Chapters 3 and 4. Ask members to read them both during the coming week, if it is possible for them to do so.

Close with prayer that God will help us grow in faith and understanding and will guide us into the practices that will help each of us grow.

SESSION FOUR

GOALS

To examine the Articles of Religion and Confession of Faith
To raise questions about doctrine in The United Methodist Church
To explore ways to find answers to those questions

MATERIALS

copies of BELIEF MATTERS
a poster-size chart, with the headings of the Articles of Religion and Confession of Faith listed in parallel columns

GETTING INTO THE SESSION

Tell the group about the historical background of the Articles of Religion and the Confession of Faith (See pages 71–73 and 99–101 in BELIEF MATTERS and pages 50–56 in *The Book of Discipline*.). You may also need to say a bit about why we have both Methodist and Evangelical United Brethren traditions in our doctrinal standards. Some people may not know that these two groups merged to become The United Methodist Church.

WORKING THROUGH THE SESSION

1. Display the poster with the headings found in the Articles of Religion and the Confession of Faith. Ask: *What similarities do you see? What are some differences?*
2. Form teams of three. Ask each team to move so there is enough space between the teams to allow them to talk without being too disruptive of others. Ask each team to select one article from the Articles of Religion (or group of articles—BELIEF MATTERS, page 73) to read and compare with the comparable article in the Confession of Faith. If there is no comparable article, ask them to speculate on why this might be the case. In addition, they should raise questions about the article and note any issues it might raise for the church today. (You may want to assign articles to teams so that they cover at least most of the Articles of Religion/Confession of Faith.)
Allow twenty minutes for this discussion. Then call the teams back together and ask for reports. As teams report questions and issues, list

these on a chalkboard or large piece of paper. Also list any questions the group may raise in response to a report.

If there is time, and you feel comfortable doing so, try answering some of the questions on the list. If you are not comfortable with that, work with the group to plan ways to find answers to the questions (Some of the resources at the end of Chapters 3 and 4 in BELIEF MATTERS would be helpful in this task.).

3. Ask: *Which of these articles deals with a topic or theme that you had never considered before? Now that it has come to your attention, what do you think about it? Why do you suppose our ancestors in the faith thought these articles were so important?*

4. Dr. Yrigoyen points out two obvious problems with the Articles from a contemporary perspective: an anti-Roman Catholic bias and the use of gender-exclusive language. Ask: *Had you noticed these problems?*

Ask: *Here's an interesting thought. If these are our standards of doctrine and we cannot change them, are we in fact denying our standards when we engage in dialogue with Roman Catholics? Or are we interpreting the standards to fit a new situation? How do you feel about that?*

5. Ask: *Dr. Yrigoyen says there are five areas of theology with which the Articles deal. What are they? How do they compare with the three areas in the* Notes *and the seven in the* Sermons? *Is something still missing for you? If so, what?*

CLOSING THE SESSION

Ask for volunteers to do research on some of the questions raised by the teams in Activity 2 above. Or, if the group came up with a different plan for finding answers, be sure that someone plans to follow through (inviting a guest expert, for example).

Close with prayer.

SESSION FIVE

GOALS

To deal with questions of faith
To clarify the "heart of the faith"

MATERIALS

copies of BELIEF MATTERS
copies of *The United Methodist Hymnal*
reports from volunteers, a guest expert, or some other method of dealing with questions from the last session

GETTING INTO THE SESSION

As group members arrive, ask them to pair off and to talk to their partner about a time when it was incredibly important for them to know what they believed about some issue or to talk about a time when they wished they had known what they believed about something.

WORKING THROUGH THE SESSION

1. Ask: **Would anyone like to tell the whole group the story about believing that you just told your partner?** (Note: If no one does, that is OK. But someone will probably want to.)

2. Follow through on whatever plan you developed last time for dealing with questions about the Articles and Confession. If persons volunteered to do research, ask them to report. If you invited the pastor or some other expert to help deal with the questions, give her or him the floor and the opportunity to answer at least some of the questions. This discussion could take most of the session, so be prepared to offer options for dealing with the material you did not get to cover.

3. Come back to the question of the heart of the faith. Point out that in Chapter 1, you talked about three doctrinal themes in the *Notes*. In Chapter 2, you found seven themes in the Standard Sermons. In Chapters 3 and 4, there is a longer list of doctrinal themes in the Articles of Religion and the Confession of Faith.

With the help of the group, list all these themes on a chalkboard or large piece of paper.

Ask: **What are the recurring themes in all the lists? Would we want to** *say that these are the heart of the faith? Does a majority vote always give a true answer? Is there a theme that is mentioned only once that is so important to you that you would always want it included, even if others showed no interest in that doctrine? Why is it so important? Is something still missing for you? If so, what is it?* (For example, some adults Dr. Yrigoyen talked with were concerned that there was nothing about creation, God working in history, or social justice in the lists.)

Ask: *What is the heart of the faith for John Wesley? What is the heart of the faith for you?*

4. Distribute copies of *The United Methodist Hymnal.* Invite the class to turn to the "Index of Topics and Categories," which begins on page 934. Tell them their task is to pick one or two of the core topics we have been talking about and to see what hymns about that topic are in our hymnal. Group members may have to look under more than one category in order to find what they are looking for, so allow plenty of time for this activity. Then ask for reports: *What did you find? How many of those hymns are familiar to you? How many do we sing regularly in church?*

5. Dr. Yrigoyen says (pages 124–25) that United Methodist theology is based primarily in the Bible and takes very seriously the tradition of the church. Ask: *On the basis of our study to this point, would you agree or disagree with that statement? For example, do the Articles and Confession stand with the Apostles' Creed and the Nicene Creed? What evidence would support your position?*

CLOSING THE SESSION

Tell the group there will be a time of silence in which you want them to reflect on what the class has learned together. Ask them to focus on ways their own faith has been enriched in this study and on new understandings of the faith they have gained.

Close with a prayer of thanksgiving.

SESSION SIX

GOALS

To deal with the "So what?" questions
To discover ways doctrine will help us in our Christian walk

MATERIALS

copies of BELIEF MATTERS

GETTING INTO THE SESSION

Tell the group that this session may be the most important of the entire study because it is the session in which we deal with the "So what?" questions.

Ask: *Are there some "So what?" questions you would like to raise about the study?* (List these questions on a chalkboard or large piece of paper, and try to deal with them in some way before the end of the session.)

WORKING THROUGH THE SESSION

1. Begin with Wesley on "think and let think" (See page 124 of BELIEF MATTERS.) Ask: *What does Dr. Yrigoyen say Wesley meant by that? What is the "root of Christianity"? If we take Wesley seriously, then what do we do about all the things that are not the "root" of Christianity? How do we live out differences on issues that are not the "root"? What did Wesley say?*

2. One of the major issues on which United Methodists disagree today is the authority of the Scriptures. Ask the group to find the Articles on Scripture. Notice that they say the Scriptures contain everything necessary for salvation. Ask: *What does that statement mean to you? Does it mean the Scriptures contain all truth on every topic? What is necessary for salvation? If we took our answer seriously, how would it help us deal with some of the issues on which we disagree in United Methodism?*

3. Ask: *What is the difference between theology and doctrinal standards?* (See BELIEF MATTERS, page 127.) *What is the function of each?* Tell the group that, on this understanding, the doctrinal standards function for us in much the same way as the historic creeds of the church. They say, in effect, "Here are the boundaries of theology. Within these boundaries you can speculate and think and disagree all you want. But if you cross the boundaries in your theological thinking, then you have moved into heresy." For example, we can consider all kinds of ways in which Jesus could be both divine and human. What we cannot do (given our doctrinal standards) is to deny either the deity or the humanity of Jesus.

4. Ask: *Is correct doctrine important? Why or why not? What does Dr. Yrigoyen mean when he says that correct doctrine is important but not sufficient? Do you agree or disagree? Why?*

5. Allow some time to struggle with the "So what?" questions on the chalkboard or large piece of paper. What are some next steps the group, or individuals in the group, need to take in order to continue dealing with these questions?

CLOSING THE SESSION

Ask: *What have you learned in this study that will help you in your Christian life? How have you grown? What new steps are you planning for yourself?* Assure the group that no one has to answer those questions aloud (though they would be welcome to); but tell them they are questions everyone should answer for herself or himself in the near future.

Close with a time of prayer for the learning you have shared, for one another, and for the disagreements that may have arisen in the group during the study.

CPSIA information can be obtained at www.ICGtesting.com
Printed in the USA
BVOW04s0840170414

350885BV00009B/140/P